ASSIGNMENT PROBLEMS IN PARALLEL
AND DISTRIBUTED COMPUTING

T0353409

THE KLUWER INTERNATIONAL SERIES
IN ENGINEERING AND COMPUTER SCIENCE

PARALLEL PROCESSING AND
FIFTH GENERATION COMPUTING

Consulting Editor

Doug DeGroot

Other books in the series:

PARALLEL EXECUTION OF LOGIC PROGRAMS
John S. Conery ISBN 0–89838–194–0

**PARALLEL COMPUTATION AND COMPUTERS FOR
ARTIFICIAL INTELLIGENCE**
Janusz S. Kowalik ISBN 0–89838–227–0

MEMORY STORAGE PATTERNS IN PARALLEL PROCESSING
Mary E. Mace ISBN 0–89838–239–4

SUPERCOMPUTER ARCHITECTURE
Paul B. Schneck ISBN 0–89838–234–4

ASSIGNMENT PROBLEMS
IN
PARALLEL AND DISTRIBUTED COMPUTING

by

Shahid H. Bokhari

Department of Electrical Engineering
University of Engineering & Technology
Lahore, Pakistan
and
Institute for Computer Applications in Science & Engineering
NASA Langley Research Center
Hampton, Virginia, USA

KLUWER ACADEMIC PUBLISHERS
Boston/Dordrecht/Lancaster

Distributors for North America:
Kluwer Academic Publishers
101 Philip Drive
Assinippi Park
Norwell, Massachusetts 02061 USA

Distributors for the UK and Ireland:
Kluwer Academic Publishers
MTP Press Limited
Falcon House, Queen Square
Lancaster LA1 1RN, UNITED KINGDOM

Distributors for all other countries:
Kluwer Academic Publishers Group
Distribution Centre
Post Office Box 322
3300 AH Dordrecht, THE NETHERLANDS

Library of Congress Cataloging-in-Publication Data

Bokhari, Shahid H.
  Assignment problems in parallel and distributed
computing.

  (Kluwer international series in engineering and
computer science ; SECS 32)
  Bibliography: p.
  Includes index.
  1. Parallel processing (Electronic computers)
2. Electronic data processing—Distributed processing.
3. Computer architecture. I. Title. II. Series.
QA76.5.B579 1987   004'.35   87-18206
ISBN 0-89838-240-8

For Ambreen

CONTENTS

List of Figures

PREFACE

This book has been written for practitioners, researchers and students in the fields of parallel and distributed computing. Its objective is to provide detailed coverage of the applications of graph theoretic techniques to the problems of matching resources and requirements in multiple computer systems. There has been considerable research in this area over the last decade and intense work continues even as this is being written.

For the practitioner, this book serves as a rich source of solution techniques for problems that are routinely encountered in the real world. Algorithms are presented in sufficient detail to permit easy implementation; background material and fundamental concepts are covered in full.

The researcher will find a clear exposition of graph theoretic techniques applied to parallel and distributed computing. Research results spanning the last decade are covered and many hitherto unpublished results by the author are included. There are many unsolved problems in this field—it is hoped that this book will stimulate further research.

Finally, for the advanced undergraduate or graduate student, this book serves as a unified presentation of a large number of graph theoretic methods. No previous knowledge of graph theory is assumed: a detailed introduction is provided in Chapter 2. This book can be used as a text in a course on parallel and distributed computing at the advanced undergraduate or graduate level. It can also be used as the core material for a seminar at the graduate level. Instructors teaching courses on applied graph theory will find it useful as a supplemental text.

ACKNOWLEDGEMENTS

I am indebted to Robert Voigt and K. E. Durrani who created congenial environments for me to write this book, at Hampton and Lahore respectively. Adnan Malik, David Nicol, Sherryl Tomboulian, Robert Voigt and Susan Voigt read through portions of the manuscript and provided me with valuable comments. Any errors that remain are, of course, my own responsibility.

I am grateful to Doug Peterson for his patience in helping me format the manuscript on his long suffering laser printer. Donald Childress at Kluwer was very helpful throughout this long project.

Finally I thank my wife Ambreen for her patience, support and understanding while I was writing this book. It would not have been completed without her encouragement.

ASSIGNMENT PROBLEMS IN PARALLEL
AND DISTRIBUTED COMPUTING

CHAPTER 1
Introduction

The assignment problem is a fundamental aspect of distributed computing. It arises whenever the procedures or modules of a program are *distributed* over several interconnected computers so that program activity moves among processors as execution proceeds. The program may be serial (only one module active on one processor at a time) or parallel (several modules concurrently active on several processors). The assignment problem deals with the question of assigning modules to processors so as to minimize the cost of running a program. The cost may be time, money or some other measure of resource usage.

1.1. The Motivations for Distributed Processing

The potential for distributed processing exists whenever there are several computers interconnected in some fashion so that a program or procedure running on one machine can transfer control to a procedure running on another. A typical distributed program structure is shown in Figure 1.1. The circles in Figure 1.1 (a) represent *modules* which are defined to be collections of procedures that can reside on different processors. Lines joining pairs of modules represent the fact that control is transferred between these modules at one or more points during the lifetime of the program. In Figure 1.1 (b) the large circles represent processors, and the long rectangles joining some pairs of processors denote interprocessor communication links. This multiple computer system is incompletely connected, i.e. not all pairs of processors have links between them.

In such an environment we wish to assign optimally the modules of a program to specific processors. Our objective in optimizing may be to minimize the running time of the program, its financial or billing cost, or some other measure of resource usage.

1.1.1. Distributed Processing of Serial Programs

Our distributed program may be serial or parallel. In a serial program only one module is active on one processor at one time, even though there are many modules and several processors.

The motivation for distributing the modules of a serial program is to take advantage of the specific efficiencies of certain processors in executing certain types of computation. Thus if our program does heavy floating point computation in one procedure and extensive symbol manipulation in another, we would execute the first procedure on a processor that has a powerful floating point unit, and the second on a processor with an instruction set especially designed for symbol manipulation.

This process can be continued for all constituent modules of the program, each module being assigned to the processor that executes it most efficiently. This is a perfectly acceptable solution if all interprocessor communication costs are zero, that is there is no overhead of passing control and parameters from a module resident on one machine to a module resident on another. Unfortunately, in most real systems this overhead is significant. In order to optimally partition the program,

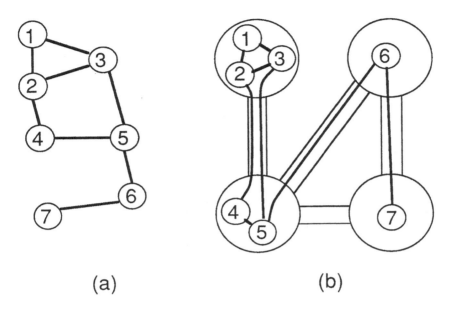

Figure 1.1 (a) Graph of a 7 module distributed program. (b) Distributed execution of this program on a 4 processor system.

we must balance the gain in running modules on specialized processors against the loss caused by interprocessor communications. Figure 1.2 illustrates the necessity of this consideration.

The above discussion assumes that we are minimizing the total time to execute our serial program. Similar arguments apply if we are minimizing the financial cost of running the program. In this case we would be billed at specific rates per unit of time for the use of each processor and each communication link.

The key issue in distributed processing of serial programs is *variability* or *non-uniformity* of computation requirements and of resources, and the overhead of communications. Non-uniformity in programs arises because different types of computation are done in different parts of the program. Variability of computational resources arises because machines have different computational capabilities or different amounts of load. Communication overhead arises because intermachine communication is significantly slower than intramachine communication. The challenge of distributed processing lies in matching requirements

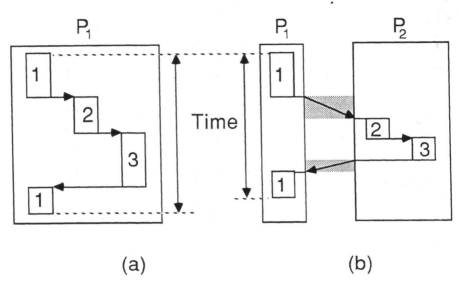

(a)   (b)

Figure 1.2 (a) A serial program executing on a single processor. Lengths of small rectangles represent the time spent executing in each module. Arrows between rectangles represent transfers of control between modules. **(b)** The same serial program partitioned over a two processor system. Processor 2 can execute modules 2 and 3 more efficiently but transfers of control between modules are over a communication link and incur appreciable overhead.

---

against resources, without incurring excessive communication overhead.

1.1.2. Parallel Processing

In the case of a parallel program, two or more modules may execute concurrently for various periods during the lifetime of the program, as shown in Figure 1.3. The objective is to reduce the total "wall-clock" time of the program by running different parts of the program in parallel. All the factors that influence the time to execute a serial distributed program also apply to parallel programs. In addition, there is the problem of scheduling the parallel computation, that is arranging the order of execution of the various modules on the processors (Coffman 76). We will not address the scheduling problem in this book.

1.2. Environments for Distributed Processing

A common application of distributed processing is in an organization that has a network of workstations or personal computers. In such an environment it is feasible to partition a single large task so as to take advantage of lightly loaded or idle processors. The problem becomes more interesting should one or more of the processors have a specialized facility, such as a powerful floating point unit.

Rapid advances in the field of computer communications (Metcalfe & Boggs 76) since the early 1970's have resulted in economical and effective techniques for interconnecting computers. An organization possessing several large computers can very cheaply connect them up into a network. In such systems it can be beneficial to split up a large program over several machines to take advantage of variability in the

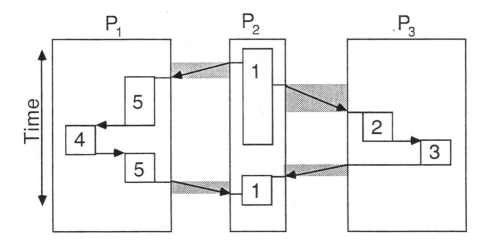

Figure 1.3 Parallel processing of a 5 module program on a 3 processor system. In this case some modules execute concurrently.

machines' power. In many cases an organization will choose to acquire computers from one manufacturer that execute the same instruction set but have widely differing power. In this case there is little difficulty in distributing a large program over the machines. However, even where the machines are different, it is possible to distribute computation if there is a standard inter-module communication scheme.

1.3. Distinction between Distributed and Parallel Processing

There is no clear agreement on this question. The distributed execution of a serial program on a network of computers can certainly be termed "distributed processing." The execution of a parallel program on a specially designed array of processors such as the Illiac-IV (Barnes et al. 68), FEM (Jordan 78), MPP (Batcher 80), or PAX (Hoshino et al. 83) would unambiguously be considered "parallel processing." But is the execution of a parallel program on a network of workstations "distributed," "parallel," or both? And what about the parallel execution of a number of independent serial programs on such a network?

We can attempt to make a distinction based on the nature of the constituent processors in a system. Thus distributed processing is what takes place on a system made up of more or less autonomous, general-purpose machines connected via a network. Such a network is called a "distributed processor system." When a parallel program is run on an interconnected collection of special-purpose machines, this is called "parallel processing," and the collection of machines is called a "parallel processor." However this definition cannot account for the many parallel processing systems that are made up of fully autonomous machines, each of which can be utilized in isolation if desired. An example of such a system is the Flex/32 (Matelan 85).

Another distinction is based on the speed of interprocessor communications. According to this definition, processing is parallel if interprocessor communications are very fast (i.e. on the order of memory access rates); processing is distributed if interprocessor communications are slow (much slower than memory accesses). This distinction breaks down when we consider the extremely high speed communications that are possible when optical media are used in computer networks designed for distributed processing, and the atrociously slow communication speeds of many parallel processors.

We will not dwell on this issue any further, as the objective of this book is not the classification of various types of processing but rather the study of how program execution can be optimized. It is enough for the reader to realize that there is no generally accepted distinction between the terms "parallel processing" and "distributed processing."

1.4. The Central Problem Addressed in this book

The central problem that concerns us is that of assigning the modules of a program to the processors of a multiple computer system. A module is taken to be a collection of procedures or subroutines, or could be one or more data files. There are bindings or linkages between some pairs of modules since a procedure in one module may wish to (1) transfer control to another procedure in a different module or (2) access data contained in a different module.

Our objective is to find an assignment that minimizes the total cost of executing the program. We will assume that the costs of assigning modules to different processors as well as the intermodule communication costs are known to us. The time required to determine these costs through experiments is justified in the case of "production" programs, i.e. those programs that run repeatedly day after day. It is exactly for these kinds of programs that the effort of finding the optimal assignment is justified in the first place.

A variant of the central problem occurs when all processors execute the same program, but on different portions of a large "computational domain." In this case we need to partition the computational domain into subdomains and to assign each to a separate processor. This is exclusively a problem of partitioning data.

1.5. Graph-Theoretic Solution Techniques

Graph theory is a branch of mathematics that has found numerous applications in many different fields (Deo 74), (Roberts 78). It deals with entities ('nodes'), connections between entities ('edges') and the consequences of these connections. Graph theoretic techniques have been successful in modeling many problems of assignment and partitioning in distributed systems. This is not surprising, since the notions of 'node' and 'edge' from graph theory are very similar to the concepts of 'module' and 'communication' in distributed programs. The idea of partitioning a program is analogous to the concept of partitioning a graph and so on.

There is usually a very clear relationship between a problem and its graph theoretic model. This gives the practitioner great insight into the structure and properties of the problem. This is in contrast with other mathematical modeling techniques where the model is essentially a set of equations or abstract algebraic structures which require deep understanding of mathematics to appreciate.

However, as elegant as it may be, the mere creation of a graph theoretic model is not enough—a solution to the required problem must also be found. For example, while it is straightforward to express a two processor assignment problem as a graph partitioning problem, only a very carefully designed graph will permit the problem to be solved using an efficient network flow algorithm. There exist many important problems that can be stated simply in graph theoretic terms but are as yet unsolved. Many of these can be shown to belong to the class of 'NP-Complete' problems that are generally considered intractable (Garey & Johnson 79).

1.6. Overview

Chapter 2 provides the reader with a survey of the basic concepts from graph theory used in the remainder of this book. Some of the more involved topics are, however, deferred to the chapters in which they are employed.

Following this introductory material, we describe in Chapter 3 Stone's network flow algorithm for finding optimal assignments in dual processor systems (Stone 77a). This chapter also describes extensions of Stone's algorithm to the problem of finding optimal dynamic assignments. Previously unpublished results by the author on the problem of optimally partitioning resources in a dual processor system are also presented.

Chapter 4 covers Bokhari's shortest tree algorithm for optimal assignments of tree structured programs (Bokhari 81b). The applications and extensions of this algorithm are discussed along with the recent results by Towsley (86) on series-parallel graphs.

In Chapter 5 we discuss the behavior of optimal assignments in dual processor systems when the load varies on one or both processors and/or on the communication link. The material in this chapter brings together the work of Stone (78), and previously unpublished results by the author.

Chapter 6 describes the sum-bottleneck path algorithm recently developed by Bokhari (87) and its many applications. This algorithm can take concurrency into account and can be used to optimally assign certain restricted classes of parallel and pipelined programs. Chapter 7 describes the mapping problem for parallel processing and the binary dissection strategy for non-uniform problems developed by Berger & Bokhari (87).

Chapter 8 concludes this book with a summary of results and a discussion of problems that remain open. This chapter also contains an overview of related research and a survey of the sources of information on distributed and parallel processing.

CHAPTER 2
Graph-Theoretic Concepts

In this chapter we introduce the reader to those concepts from graph theory that underlie the two major approaches to the assignment problem presented in this book. As discussed briefly in the introduction, these graph theoretic concepts lend themselves very naturally to the analysis of partitioning problems on multiple computer systems. As with all introductory tracts on graph theory, we must necessarily cover a substantial number of definitions before applying these concepts in an interesting fashion. The reader comfortable with graph theoretic ideas may skip over this chapter, returning as necessary to refer to specific definitions. It is, however, important for the novice to have some familiarity with these ideas before venturing into subsequent chapters.

2.1. Directed Graphs

2.1.1. Basic Definitions

Mathematically speaking, a *directed graph* or *digraph* $G=<V,E>$ consists of a set V of *vertices* or, equivalently, *nodes* and a set E of ordered pairs of these vertices called *directed edges,* or simply *edges.*

Since the edges are ordered pairs, there is a *direction* associated with each edge. Thus the edge denoted $<x,y>$ is considered to extend from node x (the *tail*) to node y (the *head*). Figure 2.1 illustrates a directed graph of 5 nodes and 9 edges. In this case
$V=\{a,b,c,d,e\}$
and
$E=\{<a,b>,<b,c>,<c,d>,<a,c>,<a,e>,<c,e>,<b,d>,<d,c>,<e,b>\}.$

Note how arrowheads are used to denote direction in Figure 2.1, and that the edges $<c,d>$ and $<d,c>$ are considered distinct.

The number of vertices or nodes in a graph, i.e. the cardinality of the set V, is usually denoted by n. Similarly, the number of edges is the cardinality of the set E and is denoted by e.

The *indegree (outdegree)* of a node is the number of edges entering (leaving) that node. The indegree of node d in Figure 2.1 is 2. Its outdegree is 1. The maximum in- or outdegree of a node in a directed graph is $n-1$. It follows that the maximum number of edges in a

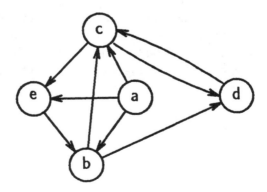

Figure 2.1 A directed graph with 5 nodes and 9 edges.

directed graph is $n(n-1)$, since each of the n nodes may be connected to all the remaining nodes.

2.1.2. Paths in Directed Graphs

A *directed path* from node s to node t in a directed graph $G=<V,E>$ is a sequence of edges $<s,p>$, $<p,q>$, $<q,r>$, ... , $<u,v>$, $<v,w>$, $<w,t>$, such that the tail of the first edge is s, the head of the last edge is t and for all except the last edge, the head of any edge coincides with the tail of the edge immediately after it.

For example, in Figure 2.1, the sequence of edges $P_1=$ $<a,b>$, $<b,c>$, $<c,e>$ forms a directed path from node a to node e. The sequence $P_2=$ $<a,c>$, $<c,e>$ forms another directed path from a to e.

We require that a node be encountered at most once as we travel down a directed path. Thus, in Figure 2.1, the edges $<b,c>$, $<c,e>$ form a path from b to e but $<b,c>$, $<c,d>$, $<d,c>$, $<c,e>$ do not, since node c is visited twice.

If s coincides with t, i.e. the path starts and ends at the same node, it is called a *cycle*. A directed graph may or may not contain a cycle. If it does not it is called an *acyclic* digraph.

The edges $<b,d>$, $<d,c>$, $<c,e>$, $<e,b>$ form a cycle in the graph of Figure 2.1.

The *length* of a path between two nodes s and t is the number of edges in that path. The paths P_1 and P_2, described above, have lengths 3 and 2 respectively.

2.2. Undirected Graphs

2.2.1. Basic Definitions

Informally, an *undirected graph* is a graph in which the edges do not have directions and no more than one edge connects a pair of nodes. There is no universally accepted notation to distinguish between directed and undirected graphs. We choose to use the same notation, i.e. $G=<V,E>$, and let the context determine whether the graph is directed or undirected. In the case of undirected graphs, V is, as before, a set of *vertices* or *nodes*. However E is a set of unordered pairs or tuples, since there is no direction associated with an edge.

To illustrate an undirected graph we have in Figure 2.2,
$V=\{f,g,h,i,j\}$
and
$E=\{(f,g),(f,h),(h,i),(j,g),(h,j)\}$.

Edges are denoted by round parentheses to emphasize the fact that no order is implied. The edges (j,g) and (g,j) would be considered the same and could not both appear in the set E. The number of nodes (edges) in an undirected graph is again denoted by n (e).

If two nodes x and y are connected with an edge (x,y), they are said to be *adjacent,* and the edge (x,y) is said to be *incident* on the nodes x and y.

The *degree* of a node in an undirected graph is the number of edges incident on it. The maximum degree of a node is $n-1$ and the maximum number of edges possible is $n(n-1)/2$, i.e. half the maximum number of edges in a directed graph with the same number of nodes.

2.2.2. Paths in Undirected Graphs

A *Path* joining node s to node t in an undirected graph is a sequence of edges (s,p), (p,q), (q,r) , . . . , (u,v), (v,w), (w,t), such that the first edge is incident on s, the last edge on t and every pair of

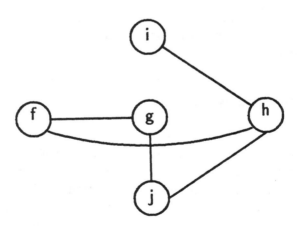

Figure 2.2 An undirected graph with 5 nodes and 5 edges.

successive edges is incident on a common node. As in digraphs, we do not allow repeated nodes in paths.

If s coincides with t the path is called a *cycle*.

The *length* of a path in an undirected graph is the number of edges in the path.

As an example, the sequence of edges (g,j), (j,h), (h,i) in Figure 2.2 forms a path of length 3 connecting nodes g and i. The edges (g,f), (f,h), (h,j), (j,g) form a cycle of length 4.

2.3. Graphs in General

We now discuss some general properties of graphs. Most of this discussion is in the context of undirected graphs which we refer to simply as 'graphs.' We will caution the reader when a definition applies specifically to directed graphs.

2.3.1. Subgraphs

A graph $G_s=<V_s,E_s>$ is called a *subgraph* of a graph $G=<V,E>$ if V_s is a subset of V and E_s is a subset of E. Of course all edges in G_s must extend between nodes in V_s.

The notion of subgraphs applies to both directed and undirected graphs. For example, the nodes V_s $=\{a,b,c,e\}$ and the edges E_s $=\{<a,c>, <a,e>, <a,b>, <b,c>, <c,e>, <e,b>\}$ form a subgraph of the graph in Figure 2.1.

A subset V_s of the nodes of a graph $G=<V,E>$ *induces* or *generates* a subgraph. This subgraph has V_s as its vertex set. Its edge set is composed of all edges from E that have both ends in V_s.

In Figure 2.1 the nodes $\{b,c,d\}$ induce a subgraph that has edges $\{<b,c>, <b,d>, <c,d>, <d,c>\}$.

2.3.2. The Underlying Graph of a Directed Graph

Given a directed graph we may choose to ignore the directions on its edges and thus arrive at a corresponding undirected graph. We will, of course, have to delete any duplicate edges joining the same pair of nodes. The resultant undirected graph is called the *underlying graph* of the given directed graph.

2.3.3. Connected Components of a Graph

A graph is called *connected* if a path exists between every pair of its nodes. A graph that is not connected (a *disconnected* graph) has two or more *components* which are simply smaller constituent graphs that are connected. The graph in Figure 2.2 is connected, as is the underlying graph of the directed graph of Fig 2.1. Figure 2.3 shows a graph with three components.

2.3.4. Cutsets

A *cutset* or *cut* of a connected graph is defined to be a subset of the edges of the graph which has the following properties.

(1) Removal of these edges disconnects the graph and

(2) No proper subset of these edges also satisfies property (1).

In Figure 2.4, for example,

(i) edges (b,c), (c,h), (d,a), (d,g), (d,h), (d,e) (indicated with a dashed line) form a cutset because their removal would disconnect the graph into two components, with nodes c and d in one component and all the remaining nodes in the other component.

(ii) edges (e,h), (d,h), (c,h), (e,f) do not form a cutset because their removal would *not* disconnect the graph.

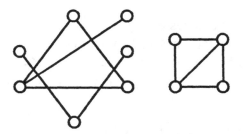

Figure 2.3 A graph with three components.

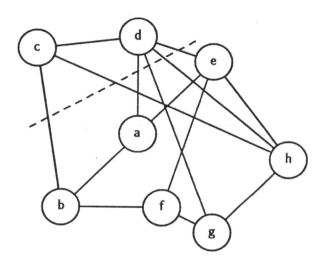

Figure 2.4 The dashed line indicates a cutset.

(iii) edges (b,c), (a,b), (a,e), (e,f), (d,g), (d,h), (c,h), (e,h) do not form a cutset because a subset of these edges can disconnect the graph (edge (a,e) is redundant).

Property (2) above states, in fact, that a cutset is a *minimal* subset of edges that must be removed in order to disconnect the graph. This is an important property of cutsets that is sometimes overlooked.

2.3.5. s-t cuts

If a graph G has two distinguished nodes s and t and if a cutset breaks G into two components G_1 and G_2 such that s is contained in G_1 and t in G_2, then the cutset is called an *s-t cut*.

When the edges of an *s-t* cut are removed from the graph, nodes s and t are said to be *disconnected* from each other.

2.4. Weighted Graphs

A *weighted graph* is one in which there is a real number associated with each edge called the *weight* of the edge. For the purposes of the discussion in this book, the weights will always be non-negative. The following definitions apply to weighted graphs.

The *length* (or *weight*) of a path in a weighted graph is the sum of the weights of all the edges in that path. A similar definition applies to directed paths in directed weighted graphs.

The *bottleneck weight* of a path in a directed graph is the weight of the *heaviest* edge in that path.

Observe first that the terms *length* and *weight* are used synonymously in this discussion. Secondly, note that the definition of bottleneck weight is the opposite of what one might intuitively expect. That is, one would expect the bottleneck weight to be the weight of the lightest edge in the graph. However, it suits our needs to define bottleneck weight as we have. Figure 2.5 illustrates these definitions. This figure shows a weighted directed graph. A weighted undirected

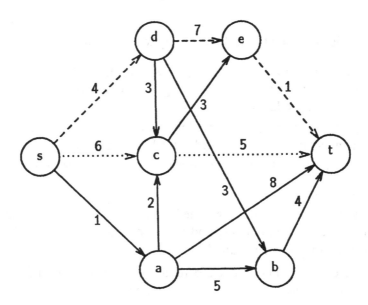

Figure 2.5 A weighted digraph. The weight of the dashed path is 12. The dotted path has weight 11.

graph would differ only in that we would be able to traverse edges in either direction. In this figure, the dashed path comprising edges <s,d>, <d,e>, <e,t> has weight=12 and bottleneck weight=7. The dotted path, made up of edges <s,c>, and <c,t> has weight=11 and bottleneck weight=6.

Another important definition is the following.

The *weight of a cut* in a weighted graph is the sum of the weights on all the edges in that cut.

Two cuts are indicated in Figure 2.6. The dashed cutset, which is composed of edges (s,d), (s,c), (a,f), (a,t), (a,b) has weight 19. The dotted cutset, made up of edges (e,t), (a,t), (b,c) and (a,b) has weight 17.

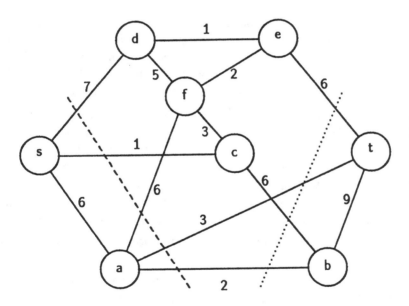

Figure 2.6 Weight of the dashed cutset is 19. Weight of the dotted cutset is 17.

2.4.1. Shortest Paths

The problem of finding the shortest path between two specified nodes in a graph will often confront us in later chapters. This is a classical problem from graph theory and was solved by Dijkstra (59). Dijkstra's algorithm can be applied to any weighted graph or digraph with positive edge weights. It will find the shortest path between the specified pair of nodes in time proportional to no worse than n^2, where n is the number of nodes in the graph*. Details of this algorithm may be found in the original paper by Dijkstra as well in a host of graph theory or combinatorial algorithm texts (Deo 74), (Lawler 76), (Hu 82), (Tarjan 83).

The shortest path between nodes s and t in the graph of Figure 2.5 is $<s,a>$, $<a,c>$, $<c,e>$, $<e,t>$, and has weight 7.

2.4.2. Mincuts

Another problem of interest to us is that of finding the *minimum weight s-t* cut or *mincut* in a weighted graph or digraph. This is again a classical problem in graph theory and we owe its solution to Ford and Fulkerson (62), who showed that this problem could be solved by finding the *maximum flow* in the network, as we now describe.

The weighted graph in which one wishes to find the minimum weight s-t cut can be viewed as a *commodity flow network*. In this interpretation, the graph is considered to be a network of pipes conveying some commodity from s to t. The weights on the edges represent capacities of the pipes. Some commodity is assumed to be flowing from node s, (the *source*) to node t (the *sink*). The source (sink) is assumed to have an infinite capacity for producing (consuming) this commodity.

The flow through the network must obey some intuitively obvious restrictions.

(1) The flow through an edge cannot exceed its capacity. An edge carrying a flow in it equal to its capacity is called *saturated*.

---

*We call this an $O(n^2)$ algorithm or say that this algorithm has $O(n^2)$ complexity. $O(f(n))$ is read "order $f(n)$." Informally speaking, an algorithm is called $O(f(n))$ if it takes time no more than $kf(n)$ to solve a problem of size n, where k is a positive constant. The reader is referred to Aho et al. (74) for a complete discussion.

(2) The flow entering a node must equal the flow leaving a node, for all nodes except s and t.

(3) node s has no flow entering it, node t has no flow leaving it and the flow leaving s must equal the flow entering t.

(4) In the case of directed weighted graphs, the flow in an edge must be in the direction of the edge.

The Ford-Fulkerson *Maxflow-Mincut theorem* states that the minimum cut in a network must equal the maximum flow. To find this minimum cut a maxflow algorithm is first applied to the network. The minimum weight cutset can easily be found by searching outwards for

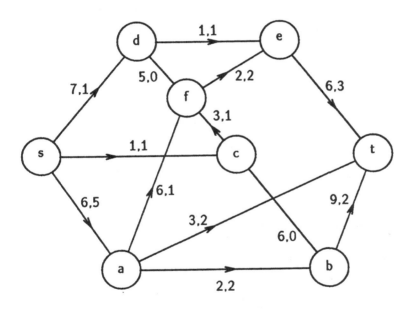

Figure 2.7 A possible flow in the graph of Fig. 2.6. The graph is undirected and arrows represent directions of flow in individual edges. Total flow leaving the source s equals total flow entering the sink t. At every other node the total flow into a node equals the total flow out. This flow is not maximum since it is possible to push more flow through (for example, through edges (s,a) and (a,t)).

unsaturated edges from the source node *s* until no further progress is possible.

Figure 2.7 illustrates an undirected weighted graph that is being considered a flow network. Each edge now has two numbers on it. The first number indicates the weight on the edge or the capacity of the edge. The second indicates the actual flow through the edge. It may be verified that the flow satisfies conditions (1), (2) and (3) above.

However this is not the maximum flow because, if we search outwards from the source, we can find a path to the sink that is composed of unsaturated edges, demonstrating that additional flow can be pushed through the network.

Figure 2.8 shows the same graph but now with the maximum flow through it. The minimum weight cut is indicated with a dashed line. It may be seen that the mincut is composed exclusively of saturated edges.

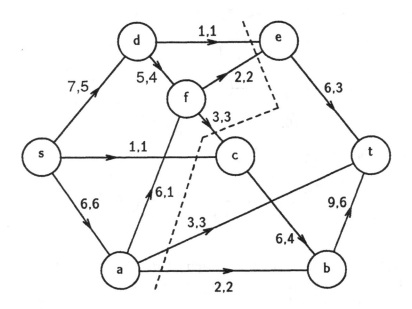

Figure 2.8 Maximum flow in the graph of Figure 2.6 is 12. The mincut (indicated by the dashed line) has weight 12.

Since Ford and Fulkerson's original work on networks there has been considerable research in finding better and better flow algorithms. The best known algorithms are those by Edmonds & Karp (72), Dinic (70) and Karzanov (74) which respectively have $O(ne^2)$, $O(n^2e)$ and $O(n^3)$ complexity, for a graph with n nodes and e edges. Many other algorithms have been developed, as discussed by Even (73,79), Hu (82), Yao (82) and Tarjan (83): these are useful only for very large, *sparse* graphs*.

2.5. Trees

A special subclass of graphs called *Trees* will be used in some of the following chapters and needs to be discussed briefly. A tree may be directed or undirected.

An undirected *tree* is a connected undirected graph which contains no cycles (Figure 2.9). An undirected tree of n nodes must *always* have $n-1$ edges because addition of any further edges would introduce a cycle. The nodes with degree 1 in a tree are called *leaf* nodes

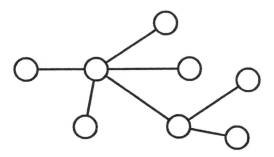

Figure 2.9 A tree.

---

*A sparse graph is one in which the number of edges is much smaller than the maximum number of edges possible.

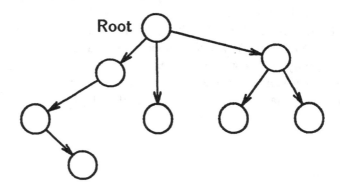

Figure 2.10 An arboresence.

2.5.1. Directed Trees

We will define a *directed tree* to be a directed graph which is acyclic and whose underlying graph is a tree. A directed tree of n nodes must also have $n-1$ edges because addition of any further edges would either introduce a directed cycle in the tree or a cycle in its underlying graph.

Of specific interest to us is the *out-tree* or *arboresence* which is a directed tree with all edges directed consistently outwards from a specially designated node called the *root*. The root has indegree zero and all other nodes have indegree exactly one. Nodes with outdegree zero are called *leaf* nodes. Figure 2.10 illustrates an arboresence.

2.5.2. Binary Trees

A *binary tree* is an undirected tree in which a designated *root node* has degree no more than 2 and all other nodes have degree no more than 3. The *height* of a binary tree is the maximum distance between the root node and any leaf node.

In a *complete binary tree* the distances from the root node to any two leaf nodes can differ by at most 1 and, other than the root, there can be no more than one node of degree 2. The height of a complete binary tree of n nodes is $\lceil \log_2(n+1) \rceil - 1$.

2.6. Multigraphs

It is sometimes useful to relax the constraint that any two nodes in a graph have exactly one edge between them. Graphs in which this is allowed are called *multigraphs*. Figure 2.11 illustrates a directed multigraph.

2.7. Further Reading

This completes our very brief review of a vast subject. We have only covered those topics from graph theory that are used in the remainder of this book, and have deferred the advanced topics to the chapters in which they are utilized.

Those interested in exploring further this fascinating topic can start with the standard texts by Berge(73), Bollobas (79), Deo (74) and Harary (69). The algorithmic aspects of graph theory are addressed by Even (73,79), Hu (82) and Tarjan (83). Burr (82) contains a collection of papers that is also likely to be of interest.

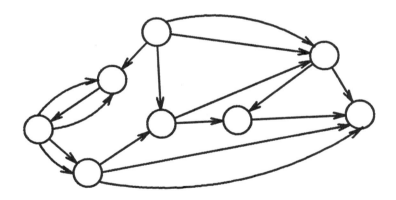

Figure 2.11 A directed multigraph.

CHAPTER 3
Network Flow Techniques

The application of network flow algorithms to assignment problems in distributed computer systems was pioneered by Harold Stone (77a). He showed how an assignment problem can be transformed into a network flow problem such that there is a one-to-one correspondence between assignments and cutsets. For the case of two processor problems, the optimal assignment—which corresponds to the minimum weight cutset—can be found very efficiently using any one of several available network flow algorithms.

We will first describe Stone's fundamental results and then go on to extensions of these results obtained by Bokhari (79). The last part of this chapter covers hitherto unpublished results on optimal assignments of resources in a dual processor system when replication is permitted.

3.1. The Basic Dual-Processor Assignment Problem

Suppose we are given a dual-processor distributed system and a distributed program made up of m modules. The two interconnected processors are independent computers with their own memories, CPUs and I/O. The modules of the distributed program may be subroutines or coroutines each capable, in general, of executing on either processor. They could also be data files that can reside on either processor. This program is called 'distributed' because its modules can reside on either processor and a module running on one processor can transfer control to a module residing on the other.

The motivation for distributing computation is to take advantage of the specific efficiency of a processor in executing certain types of computation. This can arise, for example, when one processor has a powerful floating point unit and can execute modules that perform extensive floating point computations faster than the other. It can also arise because of load conditions that cause a normally powerful processor that is time-shared among several independent jobs to perform poorly compared to the other, normally slower, processor.

A common example of this kind of situation is a host-satellite system in which a powerful host machine is connected to a modest satellite. The host is time-shared among many users, while the satellite runs in dedicated mode. Should the host have a powerful floating point unit, it is worthwhile to execute those parts of the satellite's program that involve heavy use of floating point operations on the host, and the parts that do not on the satellite. This is, however, not a simple decision since the overhead of intermodule communication over the interprocessor link also plays a part in the overall performance figures. If two modules that communicate heavily with each other are not coresident then the benefit of putting them on different processors may well be nullified by the overhead of interprocessor communication.

Our problem is thus one of splitting a program into two parts, such that the sum of all the execution costs of all modules *and* all the communication costs of all non-coresident modules, is minimum. We assume that, should two modules be resident on the same processor, the costs for intermodule communications are negligible, since all communication is through memory as opposed to an interprocessor link. Should this not be the case, the non-negligible intraprocessor communication cost can be accounted for by lumping it with execution cost.

If we are interested in minimizing the total execution time of our program, the costs would be in units of time. We may, however, be interested in costs other than time—for example financial costs. If we are charged at specified rates for CPU seconds of the host and satellite and for transmission over the link, we may reasonably wish to minimize the financial cost of running the program.

The techniques presented in this chapter can be used to minimize the execution time of serial programs (programs in which only one module is active on one processor at one time). The total time for execution in such programs is the sum of all the separate subperiods of execution and communication. This is typically the situation when a large program is distributed between a small satellite and a powerful host. In this case the host is usually time-shared among many independent programs and is thus not idle when the activity of our distributed program moves to the satellite.

3.1.1. Stone's Solution to the Assignment Problem

Stone's solution to the assignment problem starts off with the program graph of the distributed program (Figure 3.1). This graph has m nodes, each representing a module in the program. An edge between a pair of nodes indicates the fact that the corresponding modules communicate with each other one or more times during the lifetime of the program.

Communication and execution costs can be indicated on this graph as follows. Each edge is labeled with the total cost of communication between the corresponding pairs of processors (should they not be coresident) over the entire lifetime of the program. Thus if modules A and B communicate with each other at 12 points, each time taking 0.5 seconds, the edge (A,B) would be labeled with 6. Execution costs are indicated in Figure 3.1 by the ordered pair $<cost_{processor1},cost_{processor2}>$ associated with each node. Thus if module A takes 5 seconds if assigned to Processor 1 and 10 seconds if assigned to Processor 2, its label would be <5,10>. These costs are also cumulative—each number is the sum of many smaller periods of execution during the lifetime of the program.

It is clear that all information related to the assignment problem is encapsulated in Figure 3.1. Given this information, Stone proceeds to construct an *assignment graph* (Figure 3.2). This graph contains the

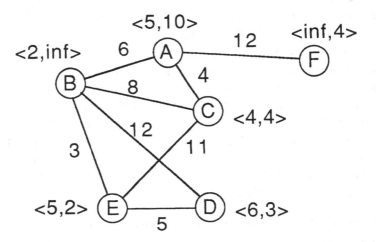

Figure 3.1 The graph of a distributed program.

program graph of Figure 3.1 and has two additional nodes and $2m$ additional edges (recall that m is the number of modules in a problem). The two additional nodes are labeled P_1 and P_2 and represent the two processors. The additional edges all extend from these nodes to the nodes representing modules. We call these *external* edges; the original edges of the program graph are called *internal* edges.

The internal edges of the assignment graph bear weights which are the same as the weights on the corresponding edges in the program graph of Figure 3.1. These represent the communication costs. The execution costs are placed on the external edges as follows. The edge connecting node i to node P_1 is labeled with the cost of executing module i on processor P_2 and vice-versa. For example in Figure 3.2, the edge joining node A and P_1 is labeled with the cost of executing module A on processor 2. This reversal of labeling is intentional—its importance will become evident in the following discussion.

Assignment graphs drawn up in the fashion described above have the following important property: a cut that disconnects P_1 and P_2 corresponds to an assignment of modules to processors and vice versa.

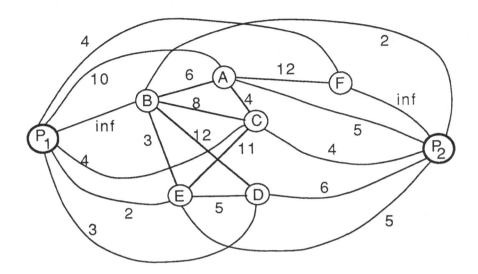

Figure 3.2 An assignment graph for the problem of Figure 3.1.

(In the terminology of Chapter 2, this is an s–t cut with $s=P_1$ and $t=P_2$.)
After removing the edges of the cut from the graph, the nodes that are
reachable from P_1 (P_2) are considered to be assigned to Processor 1 (2).
There is in fact a one-to-one correspondence between cuts and assignments.

Let us examine this claim in detail. Observe that in Figure 3.2 each
module node has two external edges connecting it directly to P_1 and P_2.
By cutting exactly one of these edges incident on each module plus
some additional internal edges, it is possible to disconnect the nodes P_1
and P_2 while keeping the module reachable from whichever of P_1 or P_2
we desire. Conversely, any cut that separates P_1 and P_2 *must* leave
every module reachable from either P_1 or P_2. If a node is reachable
from neither P_1 nor P_2, it is clear that we have removed more than a
minimal set of edges and do not have a cut. Thus there is a one-to-one
correspondence between cuts and assignments. The following theorem
is then of importance.

> **Theorem** [Stone (77a)]: The weight of a cut in the assignment
> graph is equal to the total cost of the corresponding module

assignment.

The proof of this theorem appears in the paper by Stone cited above. We will only discuss it informally here. Any cut that disconnects P_1 and P_2 in the assignment graph will cut exactly one of the two external edges incident on each module node. If the cut assigns a module to processor 1, it must cut the edge connecting that module node to processor 2. The weight on this edge is the cost of executing this module on processor 1. Thus the cost of module execution is correctly accounted for in the weight of the cut. This explains the reversal of edge weights on external edges when adding weights on the assignment graph. If two modules are assigned to different processors, the edge connecting them (if any) must be cut. This edge has weight equal to the cost of intermodule communications between these modules, should they not be coresident. This is true for all pairs of modules. The communication costs are thus also correctly accounted for in the weight of the cut.

We have shown that there is a one-to-one correspondence between assignments and cuts and the weight of a cut is equal to the cost of the corresponding assignment. It follows that in order to find the optimal or minimum cost assignment one needs to find the minimum weight cut or mincut in the assignment graph. This is done by applying a maximum flow algorithm with P_1 as source and P_2 as sink. The time taken by the algorithm is no worse than $O(m^3)$, where m is the number of modules.

3.1.2. Applications

Stone's network flow techniques were first applied to the Brown University Graphics System which was composed of an IBM 360 linked to a graphics minicomputer (van Dam et al. 74), (Foley-van Dam 82). These experiments demonstrated the applicability of this flow technique to a real world environment. At the present time many commercial computer manufacturers sell distributed systems made up of one large central machine connected through a network to dozens or even hundreds of satellite workstations or personal computers (Sun 86). The central machine serves as a number cruncher and file server while the workstations provide very fast response time for simple tasks like editing, debugging etc. In such systems the possibility always exists of partitioning a task between the central host and the workstation in order to improve performance. In Chapter 6 we will discuss how this flow approach can be extended to obtain a globally optimal assignment, i.e. one that optimizes the performance on all satellites, not just one satellite.

3.2. Memory Constraints

The solution to the assignment problem assumes that there are no memory constraints on either of the two processors so that, if need be, we may assign any number of modules to either processor. This creates no problems if both processors have enough memory to hold the entire program. This may not always be the case and it may so happen that the sum of memory requirements of the modules assigned by the optimal assignment to one or both processors exceed the available memory.

Rao et al. (79) have studied the problem of finding the optimal assignment when there is a memory constraint on one of the processors. This problem is equivalent to the "Knapsack" problem, which is NP-Complete (Garey & Johnson 79). Rao et al. have developed techniques which can, in most cases, be used to reduce the size of the problem and thus make it feasible to find the memory constrained optimal assignment by enumerating all possibilities.

3.3. Dynamic Assignments

The assignments that are obtained using Stone's network flow techniques are *static,* since they assume that once a module is assigned to a processor, it remains there while the characteristics of the computation are constant. When the characteristics of the computation change, a new assignment must be computed. By 'characteristics of the computation' we mean the ratios of the times that the program spends in different parts of the program.

This notion of characteristics needs some further examination. Suppose we have collected detailed information on a program's activity over its lifetime which, let us suppose, is 6 minutes. An assignment graph of the type shown in Figure 3.2 can be constructed from these data and an optimal partition found using the technique described above. This assignment will be the optimal static assignment. Now let us break up the six minutes worth of detailed data on this program's execution, into two 3 minute sequences and draw up *two* separate assignment graphs. If the characteristics of the computation are constant, these graphs will be identical and will yield identical assignments. If, on the other hand, the characteristics are different then the graphs will be different and may yield different optimal assignments. To take advantage of this relatively finer grained information, we will have to *relocate* certain modules after 3 minutes of execution. There will be some cost associated with this relocation. It may or may not be worthwhile to relocate modules to take the change in program characteristics into account.

We have thus brought a new dimension into the optimal assignment problem—that of relocation. Now, carrying the fine grained division process described above to the extreme will, of course, get us to the point where we start encountering individual machine instructions. Common sense tells us that it is infeasible to reassign modules at such a fine grained level. On the other hand, the discussion above clearly indicates that reassignment may be feasible at larger intervals of time.

To resolve this difficulty, we introduce the notion of the *phases* of a distributed program.

A *phase* of a distributed program is defined as a contiguous period of time during which only one module executes. During this period the executing module may communicate with any number of the remaining modules. A module *may not* be moved from one processor to another during a phase—it may be moved only *between* phases.

With each phase is associated the following information.

(1) The executing module during this phase.

(2) Run cost of this module on each of the two processors.

(3) Costs of residence of the remaining modules on each of the two processors.

(4) Intermodule communication costs between the executing module and all other modules *if they are on different processors*.

(5) Relocation cost for each module: the cost of reassigning each module from one processor to the other at the end of this phase.

Figure 3.3 shows how this information can be represented by a graph. The number of nodes in this graph equals the number of

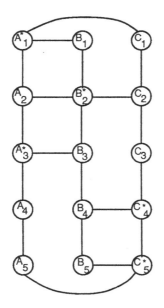

Figure 3.3 An incomplete dynamic assignment graph.

program modules multiplied by the number of phases. Each individual node represents the residence of a module in a specific phase. The single module that executes during a phase is marked with an asterisk.

The vertical edges in this graph connect successive residences of the same module and the weights on these edges equal the costs of relocating the module between the respective phases. The horizontal edges connect the executing module with other modules during the same phase and represent intermodule communication costs between the executing module and other modules during this phase.

Two distinguished nodes P_1 and P_2 can now be added to this graph as before, to represent the two processors as shown in Figure 3.4. Edges extend from P_1 and P_2 to each of the remaining nodes and are labeled with residence or execution costs. The labeling of these edges is again in the non-obvious way. The edge from node A_1 to P_1 is labeled with the cost of executing module A on processor 2 during phase 1. The residence cost of module C on processor 1 during phase 2 goes on the edge joining C_2 to P_2.

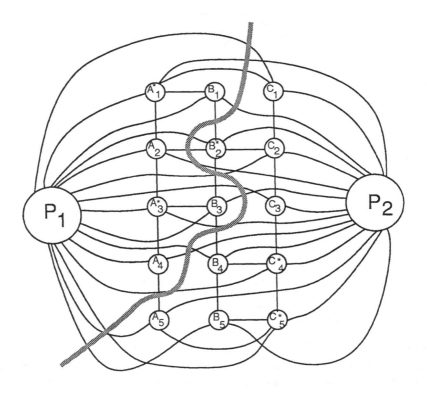

Figure 3.4 A cut in the dynamic assignment graph.

The completed graph of Figure 3.4 is called a *dynamic assignment graph*.

3.3.1. Solution to the Dynamic Assignment Problem

Inspection of Figure 3.4 will reveal that every cut that separates P_1 from P_2 in this graph corresponds to an assignment and vice-versa. The weight of the cut equals the cost of the corresponding assignment and correctly includes the costs of residence, execution, communication and, most important, relocation. This is formally proved in the paper by Bokhari (79) and we will not dwell too long on it here, except to point out how relocation costs are included.

In Figure 3.4, during phase 2, the cut indicated in the figure assigns module A to P_1 and modules B and C to P_2. During phase 3, modules A and B are assigned to P_1 and C to P_2. It can be seen that the vertical relocation cost edge joining node B_2 (which represents module B during phase 2) to node B_3 (representing module B during phase 3) is included in the cut. A vertical relocation cost edge is included in the cut whenever a relocation takes place.

Thus to find the optimal dynamic assignment of this program we need only apply a maxflow algorithm between nodes P_1 and P_2 in order to find the mincut.

3.3.2. Zero Residence Cost Graphs

The above discussion assumes that we are minimizing some abstract quantity called 'cost.' In actual fact we may wish to minimize financial cost, or time or some other measure of resource usage. Costs of residence without execution may not be of any significance in some situations. When they are not, it is possible to simplify the problem considerably by omitting all residence cost edges from the assignment graph to obtain the *zero residence cost graph* shown in Figure 3.5.

Every cut in this graph corresponds to an assignment but not vice versa since there are certain assignments that do not correspond to cuts. For example an assignment that puts B_4 on P_2 and all the remaining nodes on P_1 does not correspond to any cut in the graph (recall that a cut is a minimal set of edges that disconnects P_1 from P_2). However this creates no problems in view of the following result.

Theorem [Bokhari (79)]: For each assignment that does not correspond to a cut in the zero residence cost graph, there exists another assignment with no greater cost that does correspond to a cut.

This theorem assures us that, regardless of the lack of one-to-one correspondence between cuts and assignments, the *minimum* cost assignment will always correspond to the mincut.

The zero residence cost graph is especially important when the cost we are minimizing is execution time. In this case the notion of residence cost is not meaningful, it is the execution time of the executing module in every phase that contributes to the total time.

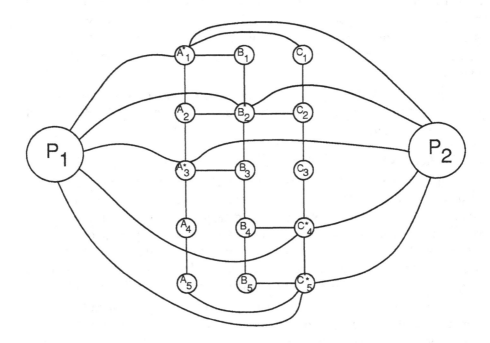

Figure 3.5 A zero residence cost dynamic assignment graph.

There are techniques for reducing the size of zero residence cost graphs that should be useful in practice. These are described in Bokhari (79).

3.3.3. Relationship between Dynamic and Static Graphs

A dynamic graph can be condensed into a static graph as shown in Figure 3.6. All pairs of nodes connected by 'vertical' relocation cost edges in Figure 3.6(a) are first merged together. This results in the multigraph of Figure 3.6(b). All edges connecting the same pair of nodes can now be merged into one edge, with weight equal to the sum of weights on the constituent edges. Figure 3.6(c) shows the end result, which is the static graph corresponding to the dynamic graph of Figure 3.6(a). For clarity, we have labeled only a few of the edges in this figure.

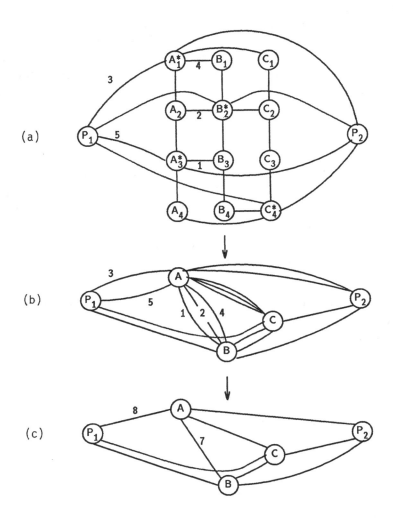

Figure 3.6 Condensing a Dynamic Graph into a Static Graph.

3.3.4. Bounds on the costs of the Dynamic Assignment

It is interesting to investigate the behavior of the optimal assignment for extreme values of relocation cost. This analysis can be done only for zero residence cost graphs.

When the relocation costs are negligible, the cut is 'horizontal' and cuts only relocation cost edges and run cost edges, as shown in Figure

3.7. This corresponds to the case where, during any phase, the executing module and all the modules that it accesses reside on the processor that runs the executing module with least cost. This assignment incurs only run costs and relocation costs—the communication costs are avoided by moving all communicating modules to the same processor. Should the relocation costs be all zero, this assignment will have minimum cost equal to

$$\sum_{\textit{all modules}} \min(\textit{run cost on } P_1, \textit{run cost on } P_2)$$

When the relocation costs approach infinity, the cut becomes 'vertical,' no module moves and no relocation cost edges are cut. In this case, which is illustrated in Figure 3.8, the cut includes only run cost edges and communication cost edges. It corresponds to a fixed assignment of modules to processors, i.e., to a static cut. A minimum weight dynamic cut will correspond to a minimum weight static cut in this case.

We can see that in the worst case the minimum weight dynamic cut is no costlier than any minimum weight static cut. In the best case it eliminates all intermodule communication.

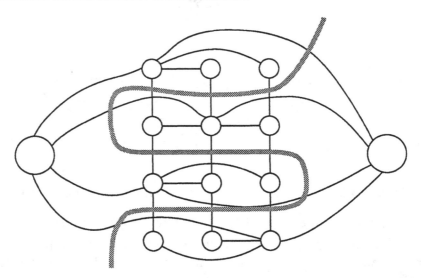

Figure 3.7 Relocation costs $\rightarrow 0$.

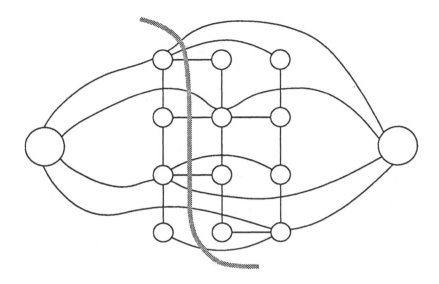

Figure 3.8 Relocation costs → ∞.

The analyses of this and the preceding section support the assertion made in Chapter 1 regarding the ease with which graph theoretic models can be manipulated to investigate the properties of the system being analyzed.

3.3.5. An Alternative Problem Formulation

In the above discussion we defined a phase to be a contiguous period of time during which only one module executes. The dynamic assignment graphs generated under this definition of phase require detailed information about program execution. In some circumstances it may not be possible to obtain such information. In other cases, we may simply not be interested in relocating at such a fine grained level, preferring instead a coarser level, for example once every 10 seconds. Furthermore, in many cases a long computation naturally breaks up into a few well defined phases based on the nature of the processing being done. It is convenient to consider relocation only between such phases.

To accommodate these cases we may revise the definition of phase as follows. A phase is a contiguous period of time during which relocation cannot take place. Modules can only be relocated between phases. The dynamic assignment graph that results when this definition is adopted is shown in Figure 3.9. Unlike the graphs discussed in the

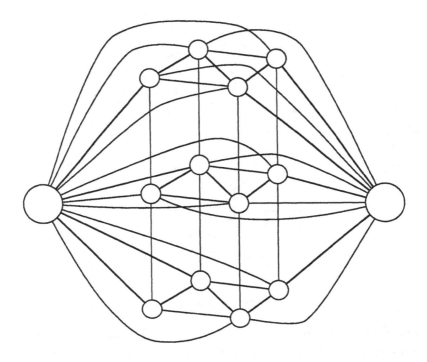

Figure 3.9 An alternative dynamic assignment graph.

previous section this graph is such that every module may execute during some time or the other during a phase. Similarly every pair of
modules may communicate during a phase. The graph of Figure 3.9 is
in fact a sequence of static graphs connected by relocation cost edges.

A mincut in this graph will correspond to the optimal dynamic
assignment and can be found using the same network flow algorithms
as before.

3.4. Resource Partitioning with Replication

We now turn to a partitioning problem that involves not only programs or program modules, but also physical resources such as line
printers, plotters etc. Suppose an organization has two computer centers
at locations that are physically separated but connected by a communication link. Then for every software or hardware resource that is
needed by the users at this organization, there can be a copy at each

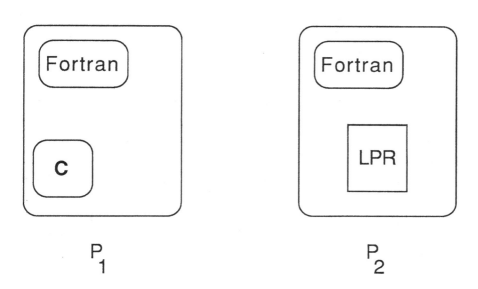

Figure 3.10 Partitioning and replicating resources between two sites.

location or just one shared copy. For example, if the line printer usage at one center is small compared to the other, only one printer need be acquired and located at the center that uses it most. The amount of usage of a proprietary Fortran compiler, for which a license fee is paid per site, may not justify two copies. One copy can be kept at one machine and accessed via a communication link from the other processor. This is illustrated in Figure 3.10.

It is clear that communication overhead plays an important part in this decision. If remote usage of the Fortran compiler grows past a certain point, it will become cost effective to acquire a second compiler, i.e. to replicate the resource. The decision to replicate the resource is influenced by the amount of remote usage, the overhead of communication and also by the 'binding' between resources. By 'binding' we mean the amount of inter-resource communication. For example, at a particular location, there may be heavy generation of compiler listings from a Fortran compiler, but not from a C compiler. There would thus be stronger bindings between the Fortran compiler and the line printer. When deciding where to assign various resources, we must keep these bindings in mind.

The problem is one of partitioning resources so as to minimize the cost of interprocessor communication and of replication. This problem can be modeled by the graph of Figure 3.11. The nodes P_1 and P_2 represent the two sites. The remaining nodes represent resources. There are two nodes for each resource, each representing the location of that resource at one of the processors. Edges between pairs of resource nodes represent costs of replication; for the case of a proprietary compiler, this would be the cost of getting a license for an extra site, for a line printer it would be the cost of acquiring a second copy.

Edges between processor nodes and resource nodes represent the usage of the resource at the processor. Thus the weight on the edge between F_1 and P_1 represents the usage of the Fortran compiler by the users on P_1. Note that the weights are not inserted in reverse order as in the previous models.

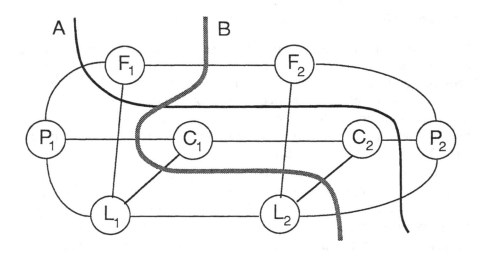

Figure 3.11 Assignment graph for a problem with replication. Nodes F_1, F_2 represent the Fortran compiler; C_1, C_2 represent the C compiler; L_1, L_2 represent the line printer.

A cut in this graph will specify an assignment with replications. For example, cut A shows an assignment that assigns all resources except the Fortran compiler to Processor 1. In this case users on P_1 would access Fortran on P_2 and incur a communication cost. This cost is correctly accounted for in the weight of the cut since the edge between P_1 and F_1 is included in the cut. Users on both machines, when generating listings from a Fortran program must send them across the link: the weight of the cut correctly includes this overhead as it includes the edges between both F_1 and L_1 (which represents the traffic due to users on P_1) and F_2 and L_2 (which represents the traffic due to users on P_2).

Cut B in Figure 3.11 includes the replication cost edge between the two Fortran nodes. This cut corresponds to an assignment that replicates the Fortran compiler—it puts the C compiler on P_2 and the line printer on P_1. While this example only shows three resources, the model can include any number, with arbitrary bindings.

3.5. Summary

We have presented network flow solutions to three problems in distributed computing. These solutions are applicable to dual processor systems. Stone (77a) has shown how the network flow model can be extended to systems made up of three or more processors. For the three processor case an algorithm that finds the minimum weight partition has been developed (Stone 77b). This algorithm works in most cases, however there are pathological graphs for which it fails to find the absolute minimum cost three way partition. For these graphs the algorithm does indicate that the solution found is not optimal and gives a bound on the amount of suboptimality. No algorithm for the case of four or more processors is known. It has, in fact, been shown that the four processor problem belongs to the class of NP-complete problems (Gursky 77).

In the next chapter we will show how this problem can be solved for any number of processors if the graph of the program is constrained in certain ways. In Chapter 6 we will discuss how the dual processor algorithm can be used to find globally optimal assignments in a single-host, multiple-satellite system.

CHAPTER 4
Shortest Path Techniques

Efficient extensions of the network flow techniques of the previous chapter to systems made up of four or more processors are not known. However, if the graph of a modular program is constrained in certain ways, it is possible to find the optimal assignment over a system made up of any number of processors in polynomial time. When the graph is constrained to be a tree, a shortest tree algorithm developed by Bokhari (81b) yields the optimal assignment. For the case of series-parallel graphs (which we will define below) an algorithm developed by Towsley (86) can be used. Both algorithms can take the speed of each processor to processor link into account. The tree algorithm can also be used to schedule precedence graphs in a distributed system in which costs vary with time so as to minimize the total cost of execution.

4.1. Introduction

Modular programs whose graphs are tree-like form an important class and include programs written as a hierarchy of subroutines. It has been suggested (Turner 80) that all large modular programs should deliberately be constructed with a tree-like structure for ease of understanding, convenience in maintenance, and high reliability.

In this chapter we first describe how a tree structured program can be assigned over a distributed system made up of an arbitrary number of processors using an efficient shortest tree approach. This solution can take into account the interconnection structure of the distributed system (i.e., the speeds of links between specific pairs of processors) a consideration that does not arise in the dual processor case. We consider this a problem of assigning across space, i.e., the space of processors. This problem and a shortest tree algorithm for its solution are described in Section 4.2. The algorithm minimizes the sum of execution and communication costs, as in the previous chapter and was developed by Bokhari (81b).

Towsley (86) has developed an efficient algorithm for solving the assignment problem for another important class of graphs called series-parallel graphs (which are defined in Section 4.3 below). This algorithm can handle program graphs in which modules lie in loops or conditional branches (i.e. there are cycles in the program graph).

In Section 4.4 we discuss how the algorithm can also be used to solve the problem of optimally scheduling a number of tasks, whose precedence relationships form a tree, over a set of processors whose costs of execution and communication vary with time. The motivation in this case is to distribute tasks over processors, delaying their execution whenever deadlines permit, so as to take advantage of periods of light loading of specific processors and communication links. We consider this a problem of scheduling across space and time.

In this case the algorithm may be used to minimize the sum of execution costs (processor and time dependent), communication costs (dependent on the characteristics of specific links and on time), and the penalties for not meeting deadlines (if any).

4.2. Assigning Trees across Space

4.2.1. Formulation of the Problem

Our problem is one of assigning modules to processors with the same objective as in the previous chapter: to minimize the sum of execution costs and communication costs. Since we will be dealing with an arbitrary number of processors, it is worthwhile to introduce some notation to succinctly describe the costs. Accordingly, we let e_{ij} denote the cost of executing module i on processor j. As in the previous chapter, each e_{ij} represents the total cost of several periods of execution of a module over the lifetime of the program (since, for example, a subroutine is typically executed several times during a program run).

The $e_{ij}'s$ for an m module, n processor problem form an $m \times n$ matrix. Since the processors are dissimilar, the cost of executing a module varies from processor to processor, that is $e_{ij} \neq e_{ik}$, in general. A module may be constrained to reside on a subset of available processors (perhaps on only one processor) by making its execution costs on the complementary subset infinite.

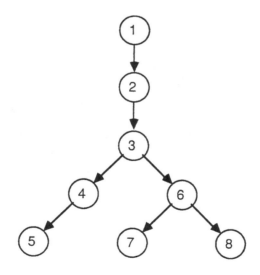

Figure 4.1 An invocation tree.

Figure 4.1 shows a the tree like program graph for the class of problems that we deal with in this Section. We call this an *invocation tree*, (it is in fact an arboresence) since it represents the way modules in the program invoke each other. Program activity starts in module 1. At one or more points during the execution of the program, module 1 invokes module 2, which in turn invokes module 3. Module 3 invokes two modules, 4 and 6. This 'branching' of program activity corresponds to two or more sets of calls in the body of module 3, some to module 4 and some to 6.

Thus, the edge joining two nodes in the tree indicates, in general, that the module represented by the ancestor node calls the descendant

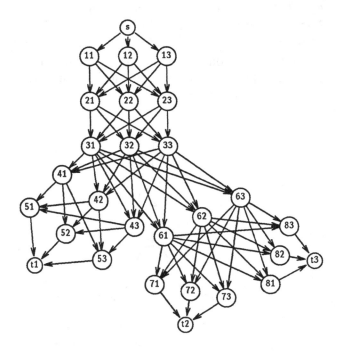

Figure 4.2 An assignment graph for the tree of Figure 4.1 and a three-processor system. There are two forksets in this graph: {31,32,33} and {61,62,63}.

node *many times* during the lifetime of the program. (A precedence ordering on module execution is *not* implied in the present discussion—we will examine that case in Section 4.4.) Should a module resident on one processor invoke a module resident on another, there will be the overhead of interprocessor communication. This will depend on the amount of data transmitted and the cost per bit of transmission between the two processors on which the modules are resident.

The total amount of data transmitted during the lifetime of the program between a module i that calls a module j is denoted by d_{ij}. The cost of transmitting this data between processors p and q is given by the function $S_{pq}(d_{ij})$. It is up to us to select this function, which can reflect the specific characteristics of the behavior of the communication link between processors p and q. Its simplest form is $S_{pq}(d_{ij}) = s_{pq} \cdot d_{ij}$ where s_{pq} is the cost of transmitting a unit amount of data between processors p and q.

We assume that $S_{pq} = S_{qp}$, i.e. the communication cost function is symmetric. This assumption permits us to associate the sum of all data flow between modules i and j (whether from i to j or j to i) with the direction i to j. Although the case $S_{pq} \neq S_{qp}$ would be quite unusual, the algorithm described below can easily be modified to handle it. (Separate $d_{ij}'s$ and $d_{ji}'s$ will be required.)

The cost of transmitting data between coresident modules is assumed to be zero, i.e., $S_{pp}=0$. This assumption can also be relaxed to account for nonnegligible intraprocessor communication costs.

There is a nonzero d_{ij} associated with each directed edge from node i to node j in the invocation tree of our program. This represents the data that must be transmitted from one module to another in order to transfer control.

4.2.2. The Assignment Graph

Given the invocation tree of Figure 4.1, and the execution and interprocessor communication costs, we can draw up an *assignment graph* as shown in Figure 4.2. This figure assumes a three-processor system.

The following definitions apply to this assignment graph.

(1) It is a directed graph with weighted edges.

(2) There is one distinguished node called the source node, denoted s.

(3) There are several *terminal nodes* t_1, t_2, $\cdots$ one for each leaf node of the invocation tree.

(4) In addition to the source and terminal nodes there $m \times n$ further nodes in the assignment graph (for a problem with m modules and n processors). Each node is labeled with a pair of numbers (i,j) and represents the assignment of module i to processor j.

(5) Each *layer* of the assignment graph corresponds to a node of the invocation tree. For example the layer comprising nodes $(2,1)$, $(2,2)$ and $(2,3)$ corresponds to node 2 of the invocation tree.

(6) Nodes in the layers corresponding to nodes in the invocation tree having outdegree greater than 1 are called *forknodes*. Each layer of

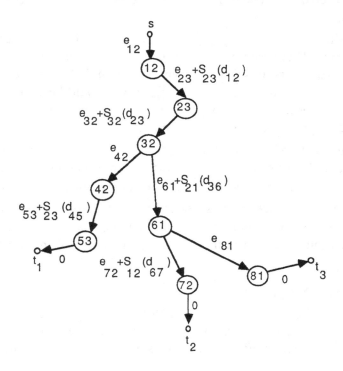

Figure 4.3 An assignment tree from Figure 4.2 shown in isolation with its edges labeled with their weights.

forknodes is called a *forkset*.

The edges of the assignment graph have weights on them according to the following rules.

(7) All edges incident on the terminal nodes t_1, t_2, etc. have zero weight on them.

(8) The edges joining source node s to nodes (1,1), (1,2), $\cdots$ have weights e_{11}, e_{12}, $\cdots$.

(9) The edge joining node (i,p) to node (j,q) has weight $e_{jq}+S_{pq}(d_{ij})$. For example, the weight on the edge joining node (1,3) to (2,1) is $e_{21} + S_{13}(d_{12})$. This equals the cost of assigning module 2 to processor 1, given that module 1 has been assigned to processor 3.

It follows from definition (4) that to each assignment of the m modules to the n processors there corresponds some subset of nodes of the assignment graph. The subgraph generated by these nodes plus the

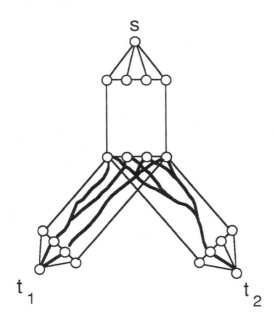

Figure 4.4 Shortest paths from t_1 and t_2 to all nodes in the forkset.

source and terminal nodes is called an *assignment tree* and has the following properties.

(1) It is an arborescence with root s.

(2) All the terminal nodes t_1, t_2, t_3, $\cdots$ of the assignment graph are leaf nodes of the assignment tree.

(3) It contains one and only one node from each layer of the assignment graph.

It is easy to see that each assignment tree corresponds to an assignment. Each assignment corresponds to an assignment tree: this is the subgraph of the assignment graph induced by the nodes corresponding to the assignment plus s and all the terminal nodes. Thus there is a one-to-one correspondence between assignment trees and module assignments. Furthermore, the weight of each assignment tree (i.e., the sum of the weights of all the edges in it) equals the cost of the corresponding assignment. This follows from property (9) of assignment graphs. Figure 4.3 shows an assignment tree from Figure 4.2.

To find the minimum cost assignment we need to find the minimum weight assignment tree in the assignment graph. This may be done using the shortest path approach described in the following section.

4.2.3. The Shortest Tree Algorithm

At the heart of the shortest tree algorithm is a procedure that will find the shortest paths from a terminal node of the assignment graph to all nodes in the nearest forkset (Figure 4.4). This may be done using a simple shortest path algorithm in $O(kn^2)$ time, where k is the number of layers between the terminal node and the forkset involved. The layered structure of this graph permits this procedure to be faster than Dijkstra's shortest path algorithm, which would take $O(k^2n^2)$. The procedure s called SHORT; it leaves pointers from each node to the next node in the shortest path to the terminal node.

We will call a forkset 'exposed' when the shortest paths from its nodes to all possible nodes have been found.

Figure 4.4 shows an assignment graph just after the application of procedure SHORT to terminal nodes t_1 and t_2. In Figure 4.5 we have temporarily removed the two limbs of the graph and created a pseudoterminal node t_0.

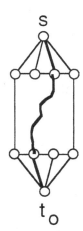

Figure 4.5 Transformed graph with shortest path from pseudo-terminal node t_0 to s.

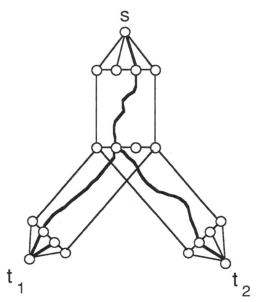

Figure 4.6 The shortest assignment tree.

Shortest Assignment Tree Algorithm
begin
>   input graph;
>   { *TSET* is the set of all terminal nodes }
>   { *FSET* is the set of all forksets }
>   **while** *TSET*>1 **do**
>> **begin**
>>>   to each terminal node *t* in *TSET* apply procedure
>>>   SHORT and remove *t* from *TSET* ;
>>>   **for** each exposed forset *f* in *FSET* **do**
>>>> **begin**
>>>>>   temporarily disconnect all outgoing edges;
>>>>>   create a pseudoterminal node t_f ;
>>>>>   join all nodes in *f* to t_f with edges that
>>>>>   have weights equal to the *sum* of the
>>>>>   several shortest paths to the several
>>>>>   discarded terminal nodes;
>>>>>   remove *f* from *FSET* ;
>>>>>   add t_f to *TSET* ;
>>>> **end**;
>> **end**;
>   find the shortest path from the last terminal node to *s* ;
>   {length of this path equals weight of shortest tree}
>   reconnect all disconnected edges;
>   traverse graph from *s* to all terminal nodes by following
>   pointers set up by procedure SHORT;
>   {each node encountered is part of the shortest tree}
end.

The weight on the edge joining t_0 to a node in the forkset equals
the sum of the shortest paths from that node to t_1 and t_2 from Figure
4.4. After finding the shortest path from s to t_0 we reconnect the two
limbs of the graph to obtain the shortest tree as shown in Figure 4.6.

This algorithm is applicable to assignment graphs derived from any invocation tree. Each application of procedure SHORT takes $O(kn^2)$ time. The total time is $\sum_i O(k_i n^2)$, where i represents each application of procedure SHORT. This equals $O(n^2)\sum_i k_i = O(mn^2)$ since the total number of layers in the graph is m.

4.3. Assigning Series-Parallel Graphs

Donald Towsley (86) has recently solved the problem of finding the optimal assignment over any number of processors of a modular program whose interconnection structure is a series-parallel graph. In this section we will define series-parallel graphs and show how an assignment graph can be constructed that includes all costs related to the problem. An *allocation graph* is a subgraph of this assignment graph that is analogous to the assignment tree of Section 4.2: there is a one-to-one correspondence between graphs and assignments.

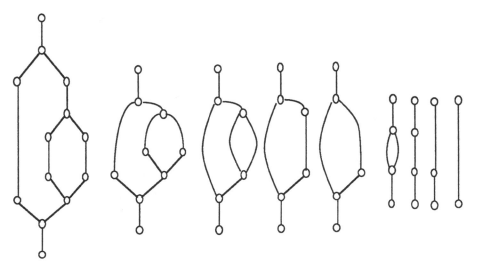

Figure 4.7 A series parallel graph and its transformation into a single edge

Towsley has shown how to find the optimal allocation graph using a series of graph transformations. Our presentation of his algorithm uses a shortest path approach similar to the one for assignment trees in Section 4.2.3. The end result in either case (whether using graph transformations or the path approach) is the same: identification of the optimal assignment. However, the path approach allows us to build on the material presented in the previous Section and makes our exposition somewhat easier.

4.3.1. Definitions

A series-parallel graph is an undirected multigraph which has two distinguished nodes called the source (s) and the sink (t), and which can be transformed into a graph with just these two nodes (s and t) connected by a single edge, by repeated applications of the following replacement rules.

(1) If two nodes have two parallel edges between them, replace these edges by one edge.

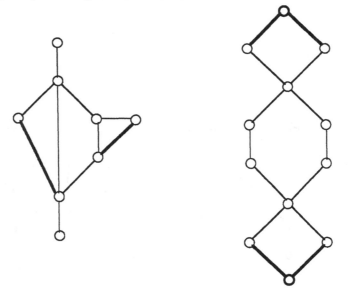

Figure 4.8 Transforming graph into series-parallel graphs by adding dummy nodes and edges (bold lines).

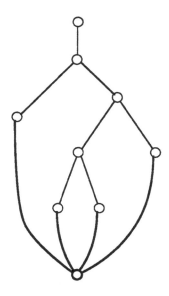

Figure 4.9 Transforming a tree into a series-parallel graph.

(2) If a node b with degree 2 is adjacent to two nodes a and c, replace b and the edges $(a,b),(b,c)$ with the single edge (a,c).

Figure 4.7 shows a series-parallel graph and its transformation into a single edge. The reader can verify with a little experimentation that the above definition restricts the number of nodes with degree 1 to be no more than 2. If such nodes exist, they must be the source and/or the sink, otherwise the graph cannot be considered series-parallel.

Although a series-parallel graph has been defined to be a multigraph, it does not necessarily *have* to contain parallel edges. However, while undergoing the transformation into a single edge, it may become a multigraph, as happens in Figure 4.7.

Some graphs can be transformed into series parallel graphs by adding suitable dummy nodes and/or dummy edges, as shown in Figure 4.8.

A tree can be transformed into a series-parallel graph by connecting all leaf nodes to a dummy node (Figure 4.9). A graph that is not series parallel, nor can be made series parallel by adding nodes and edges is shown in Figure 4.10.

Figure 4.10 A graph that is not series-parallel nor can be made series-parallel by adding nodes and edges.

We define a *spindle* to be a subgraph of a series-parallel graph that is composed of two or more paths connecting nodes x and y. These paths can have no edges in common (i.e. they are *edge disjoint*) and no nodes in common (except x and y).

A *chain* is a subgraph of a series-parallel graph composed of two nodes x and y connected by exactly one path.

Figure 4.11 illustrates these definitions. We will always draw our series-parallel graphs with the source node at the top and the sink at the bottom, with the remaining nodes arranged in such a way that we always move downwards when traversing any path from s to t. In graphs that have been drawn according to this rule, we can always refer to the nodes x and y described above as the 'top' and 'bottom' nodes of a spindle or chain.

Series parallel graphs can model the interconnection structures of some classes of programs that have loops or conditional branches in them, as discussed by Towsley (86).

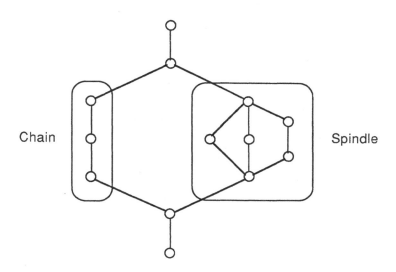

Figure 4.11 Illustrations of spindle and chain.

4.3.2. The Assignment Graph

Suppose we are given a program with m modules which has an interconnection structure that is series-parallel (or can be made series-parallel by adding dummy nodes and edges). We wish to assign this program over an n processor system. The costs associated with execution and communication are exactly the same as those defined in Section 4.2.1. Thus we have e_{ij}'s that specify the cost of executing module i on processor j, d_{ij}'s that represent the amount of data transmitted between modules i and j, and communication cost functions $S_{pq}(d)$ that define the cost of transmitting d units of data between processors p and q.

It is convenient to assume that the source s and the sink t of the program graph are dummy modules with zero communication costs. The amount of data transmitted between these nodes and others is zero. We can always add these such dummy nodes to the actual program graph. We can draw up an assignment graph as shown in Figure 4.12 for the program graph of Figure 4.7 and a three processor system. This graph is similar to the assignment graph for trees described in Section

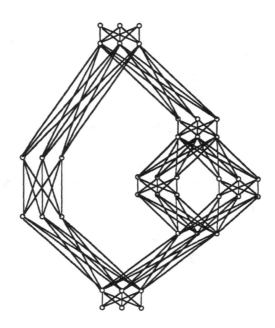

Figure 4.12 An assignment graph for the program of Figure 4.7 and a three processor system.

4.2.2. The following definitions apply to this graph.

(1) It is an undirected graph with weighted edges.

(2) It has $m \times n$ nodes (for a problem with m modules and n processors). Each node is labeled with the pair (i,j) and represents the assignment of module i to processor j.

(3) Each layer of this graph corresponds to a node in the program graph. The layer corresponding to the source (sink) is called the source (sink) layer.

(4) A part of the assignment graph corresponding to a chain (spindle) in the assignment graph is called a chain (spindle) limb (Figure 4.12).

The edges of the assignment graph are given weights according to the following procedure.

(5) All edges incident on the sink layer are given zero weight.

(6) All edges joining the source layer to the nodes $(i,1)$, $(i,2)$, $\cdots$. are given weights e_{i1}, e_{i2}, $\cdots$.

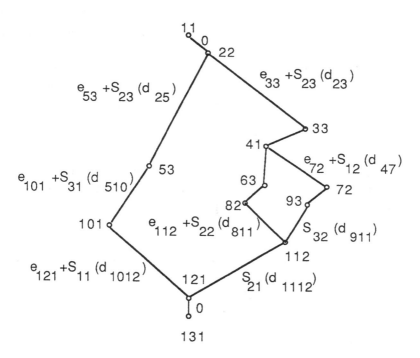

Figure 4.13 An allocation graph from the assignment graph of Figure 4.12. To avoid a congested diagram, only some of the edges have been labeled.

(7) Communication costs are accounted for by giving the weight $S_{pq}(d_{ij})$ to the edge joining node (i,p) to node (j,q).

(8) Execution costs are now *added* to the weights assigned in the previous step.

(a) If node i of the program graph has degree 2, add e_{ij} to all nodes (i,j) in layer i of the assignment graph.

(b) If node i of the program graph is the top node of a spindle add e_{ij} to all nodes (i,j) in the spindle layer i of the assignment graph.

(c) If node i of the program graph is the bottom node of a spindle, the nodes in the corresponding spindle layer will have edges incident on them from several layers above them. Add e_{ij} to the weights of *all* edges extending to layer i from any *one* layer above it.

The assignment graph is constructed in such a way that the sub-graph induced by selecting one node from each layer corresponds to an assignment. This subgraph is called an allocation graph (Figure 4.13). The weight of an allocation graph equals the cost of the corresponding assignment. This is due to the method of adding weights to the edges of the graph (Steps 8 (a),(b) and (c) above).

4.3.3. Finding the Optimal Assignment

We will now present an algorithm that finds the minimum weight allocation graph and hence the optimal assignment. This algorithm proceeds in a fashion very similar to the transformation of a series parallel graph into a single edge (Figure 4.7).

Shortest Allocation Graph Algorithm
begin
    while there is a spindle limb in the assignment graph **do**
        begin
            apply PARALLEL-SHORT to this spindle limb;
            save the shortest paths for future reference;
            replace the spindle with two layers and put weights on
                the edges between these layers equal to the shortest
                path combination between the corresponding nodes;
        end
    {the graph has now been reduced to a single chain limb}
    find the shortest paths between the top and bottom
        layers of this chain limb;
    select the lightest path: this corresponds to the
        optimal allocation graph;
    the allocation graph itself is found by combining
        the shortest paths between the selected nodes
        that were saved earlier;
end.

In a chain limb with k layers, we can find the shortest path from *every* node in the top layer to *every* node in the bottom layer in $O(kn^3)$ time using a straightforward extension of procedure SHORT from Section 4.2.3.

In a spindle limb, we can separately find for each constituent chain limb the shortest paths from each node in the top layer to each node in the bottom layer. These paths can be combined to obtain n^2 sets of shortest path combinations (one for each choice of top and bottom nodes) with total weight equal to the sum of the constituent paths. This is illustrated in Figure 4.14. Let us call this procedure PARALLEL-SHORT and assume that it returns the weights of the n^2 sets of shortest path combinations as well as the shortest paths themselves.

If our program graph is just a spindle, all we have to do is select the lightest of these n^2 shortest path combinations. In general, our program graph will contain many chains and spindles. We will proceed by replacing each spindle limb with a chain limb as described below.

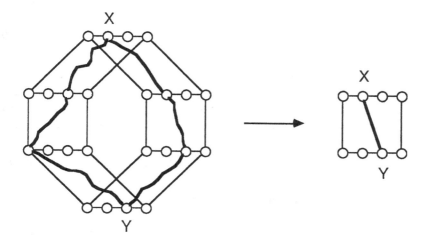

Figure 4.14 Illustration of procedure PARALLEL-SHORT which reduces a spindle limb to a chain limb. The sum of the weights on the two shortest paths between X and Y in the spindle limb is put on th edge joining X and Y in the chain limb.

This algorithm has complexity $\sum_i O(k_i n^3)$ where k_i is the number of layers in the *ith* chain limb. This equals $O(mn^3)$ since the total number of layers is m.

4.4. Optimal Assignments across Space and Time

4.4.1. Motivations

We now discuss how a set of tasks that must be executed according to a tree-like precedence relationship may be optimally scheduled over a distributed processor system in which costs vary with time. In this case an arboresence describes the relationships between tasks. A directed edge from task i to task j implies that task i must complete before task j is started. This problem is relevant to the many organizations whose computational resources are in the form of a distributed computer network with each computer servicing one or more high priority local tasks and retaining the capability of servicing remotely submitted tasks at a low priority. In a production environment, the loads on the computers are fairly predictable as they depend heavily on the specific local loads on the machines.

In such an environment we would like to distribute a large set of tasks over the system so that it utilizes whatever processors are lightly loaded. Since the loads on the processors are time dependent, we may wish to consider suspending some tasks until a time when the loads on a particular processor are very light. Some tasks may be time critical and not admit any such suspension. Our problem is one of distributing a set of tasks over a set of processors, taking into account

(1) the run cost of each task on each processor (time-dependent in general),

(2) the intercommunication costs between pairs of tasks, which depend on the pair of processors to which these tasks are assigned and may also be time dependent, and,

(3) the penalties for not meeting deadlines for tasks (which may be set to infinity if a task must be executed by a certain time).

Our objective is to minimize the cost of executing the program and not the time to execute the job. An example of such scheduling is the execution of a long engineering computation (comprising several steps to be executed) at a large computation laboratory with several computers, some of which are used for real-time computation during the day. An engineer carrying out such a calculation will often do the initial data preparation during the day and then suspend the job until night time when in may be run at very low cost on a lightly loaded machine. The final interactive examination of the results is done on the following day. Other examples are given in Bokhari (81b).

4.4.2. Formulation of the Problem

Suppose there are n processors in our system. The costs of executing tasks on processors vary with time but remain constant over specified periods of time called *phases*. This is illustrated in Figure 4.15 where the vertical axis represents the space of processors and the horizontal axis represents time. During some phases a processor may be totally unavailable because of complete dedication to a real-time task or perhaps because of scheduled maintenance.

Once a task starts executing during a particular phase, it is allowed to run to completion even if the phase ends during task execution. The time to execute a task is considered to be small compared with the length of the phase. A task that is initiated near the end of a phase is treated like a customer who arrives at a bank just before closing time— he is allowed to complete his transaction even though it extends beyond closing time.

The graph superimposed on Figure 4.15 shows one possible way of scheduling a precedence tree of tasks over the two dimensions of space (processors) and time (phases).

In the usual fashion, each node of the precedence tree represents a task and a directed edge from node i to node j implies that task i must be completed before task j is started.

The execution costs are in the form of a three dimensional matrix in which each element e_{ijk} represents the cost of executing module i on processor j during phase k. This cost will vary across the processors and phases. It may be set to infinity for some processors during certain phases if these processors are not available during these specific phases.

The penalties for not completing tasks are in the form of a two-dimensional matrix in which each element F_{ik} represents the penalty for not completing task i by the end of phase k. F_{ik} may be set to infinity

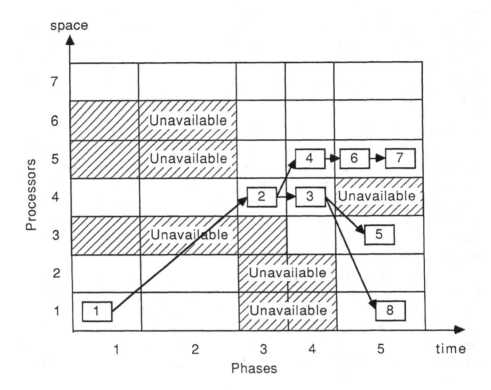

Figure 4.15 Scheduling a precedence tree over space and time.

if task i must finish by phase k.

With the edge connecting nodes i and j in the precedence tree, we have d_{ij}—the amount of data that must be transmitted between the tasks when invoking task j at the end of task i. The overhead of invoking task j in phase ϕ_w on processor p_y after completing task i in phase ϕ_v on processor p_x is a function $T(d_{ij}, p_x, \phi_v, \phi_w)$. This function can take into account (1) the amount of data transmitted, (2) the cost per bit of the link between p_x and p_y, and (3) the overhead of suspending a task when it finishes in ϕ_v and resumes in ϕ_w. A simple function, which ignores (3) above is $T=S_{xy} \cdot d_{ij}$ where S_{xy} is the cost of transmitting a unit of data between processors p_x and p_y.

4.4.3. Solution

The precedence tree of tasks described above may be scheduled to minimize the sum of execution costs, interprocessor communication costs, penalties for not meeting deadlines, and costs of suspending and resuming tasks. The solution technique is very similar to the optimal assignment approach of the previous section and is described in Bokhari (81b). A problem with m tasks, n processors and ϕ phases is formulated as the tree assignment problem of Section 4.2 with m modules and $n\phi$ phases. It can thus be solved in $O(mn^2\phi^2)$ time.

4.5. Summary

In this chapter we have discussed an efficient algorithm for assigning tree structured programs over multiple processor systems with any number of machines. This algorithm can also be used for scheduling a tree structured precedence graph over space and time. Towsley's results on assigning series-parallel graphs are a recent and very significant development and are likely to find many applications.

CHAPTER 5
Varying Load Conditions

Many distributed processing applications involve programs that run repeatedly day after day. This happens, for example, in graphics applications where a standard set of routines is used in a production environment. This is also the case in industrial process control and monitoring applications, where real-time programs execute continuously. In these cases the execution and communication costs of the various parts of the program are known accurately and an optimal assignment can be computed well before the actual running of an application.

However if one or more of the processors on which a distributed program is running is time-shared with other applications, the optimal assignment will change each time the load on one of the processors changes. This is because as more and more load is put on a processor, the time for executing modules resident on it increases. The optimal assignment at a new value of load may dictate that some modules be relocated between processors.

In this chapter we will examine this problem for the case of dual processor systems. Stone (78) has shown that, should the load on only one processor vary, there can be no more than $m+1$ different assignments for a problem with m modules. These assignments can be found and stored ahead of time and the optimal assignment for any value of load can then be determined very rapidly without having to run a flow algorithm.

When load varies on *both* processors, Carstensen (83) has shown that the number of possible optimal assignments may be exponential in m. An algorithm for finding these assignments has been developed by Gusfield (83). The author's experience with this problem indicates that the number of distinct assignments encountered in practice is small, usually lying between m and m^2. Once these assignments have been found and stored, the optimal assignment for any load condition can be found quickly using an efficient look-up technique.

The two problems mentioned above are solved under the assumption that the cost of intermodule communication is constant and independent of load conditions. When the communication cost also varies with load, the problem gets more complicated. However we will show that it is possible, even in this case, to identify and store assignments in advance so as to be able to rapidly reassign modules when the need arises.

The results on varying load conditions on both processors and those on varying communication costs have not been published previously.

5.1. Varying Load on one Processor

5.1.1. Formulation

When one of the processors in a dual-processor distributed system is time-shared, so that it services several independent jobs in addition to our distributed program, the optimal assignment is sensitive to variations in the load. Our intuition tells us that if the time-shared machine, say P_1, is heavily loaded, the optimal assignments will be such that most modules tend to reside on the other machine P_2. As the load on the time shared machine decreases, modules will tend to move from P_2 onto P_1. We model variations in the load of a machine by multiplying the costs of executing modules on it by a *load factor f*. This load factor varies between some f_{min} and f_{max}. f_{min} represents the case where P_1 has no other load on it, and can devote all of its CPU cycles to our distributed program. f_{max} represents the heaviest load conditions on P_1. The execution cost of any module i is then $e_i f$. In the mathematical analysis that follows, f will be assumed to vary from 0 to ∞. In actual practice it will, of course, vary within a range $f_{min} \cdots f_{max}$.

5.1.2. Critical Load Factors

The execution of a distributed program on a dual processor system in which the load on one processor varies is modeled by the graph of Figure 5.1. This graph is similar to the assignment graphs of Chapter 3. There is one important difference—the execution costs of modules on P_1 are not real, positive numbers but expressions of the form $e_i f$. To find the optimal assignment at any specific value of f, we substitute for f on all the edge weights and then run a flow algorithm as described in Chapter 3.

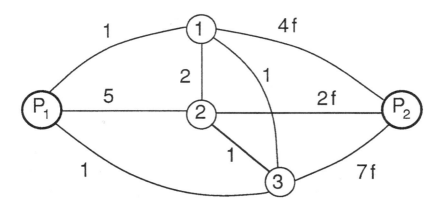

Figure 5.1 Assignment graph for a one-dimensional problem. f denotes the load on processor 1.

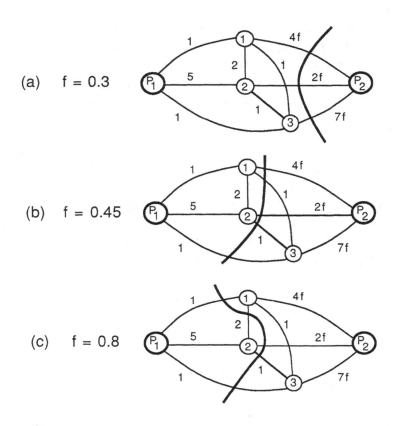

(a)   f = 0.3

(b)   f = 0.45

(c)   f = 0.8

Figure 5.2 The assignment problem of Figure 5.1 solved for **(a)** f=0.3, **(b)** f=0.45, and **(c)** f=0.8.

This is done in Figure 5.2 for f=0.3, 0.45, and 0.8. At f=0.3, the optimal assignment places all modules on P_1. At f=0.45 module 3 is assigned to P_2 and modules 1 and 2 to P_1. Finally, at f=0.8 modules 1 and 3 are assigned to P_2 and module 2 to P_1. We can easily see that if f were to increase to ∞, all modules would be assigned to P_2 since the mincut would avoid all edges with infinite weights. The sequence in which the modules move away from P_1 as the load on it increases is important to appreciate. All movement is away from P_1 and towards P_2 and *in that direction only*. In other words, successive optimal assignments are nested. At no point does a module move onto the processor on which load increases. This is a very important property that was observed in real distributed programs by Michel and van Dam (76) and was proved to hold for all assignment graphs by Stone (78). We will call it the Nesting Theorem in the following discussion.

The Nesting Theorem implies that there exists for each module i a *critical load factor* f_i such that if the load is less than f_i, i is assigned to P_1 and if it is greater than f_i, it is assigned to P_2. These critical load factors make it very easy to the find the optimal assignment at any value of load.

Figure 5.3 shows a plot of assignment weights against f, the load on P_1, for the problem of Figure 5.1. This problem has 3 modules and there are thus a total of $2^3=8$ possible assignments, the cost of each of which is plotted in this figure. We denote each assignment by enumerating the set of modules that it assigns to processor P_1. Thus {2,3} stands for the assignment that assigns modules 2 and 3 to P_1.

To find the optimal assignment for any value of load, we can erect a perpendicular to the f (horizontal) axis at that value. The first line intersected when traveling upwards will be the optimal assignment for that value of load. We have shown three such perpendiculars on Figure 5.3, corresponding to the three cases shown in Figure 5.2. The optimal assignments in this example are the four lowermost lines in this plot. No matter how the load varies, only the cuts represented by these four lines can be optimal. We say that the envelope or *convex hull** formed by these lowermost lines determines the optimal assignments. The remaining lines are of no interest to us, since they represent assignments that can *never* be optimal. Furthermore, the end points of the line segments making up this hull correspond to the critical load factors (these are approximately 0.43, 0.5 and 1.0 for modules 3, 1 and 2, respectively).

5.1.3. Applications

To find the optimal assignment at any f we do not really have to carry out the geometric construction described above. (This would be a very expensive algorithm as it would need the evaluation of 2^m expressions.) The application of a network flow algorithm achieves the same

---

*A region is called convex if a line joining any two points inside it lies wholly within the region.

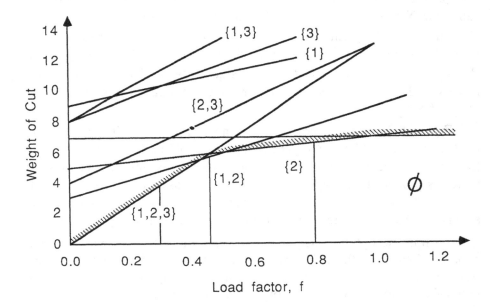

Figure 5.3 Plots of assignment weights for all assignment from Figure 5.1. Shaded envelope is the convex hull of optimal assignments.

end in no more than $O(m^3)$ time. The flow algorithm alone cannot, however, efficiently find the hull (and thus the critical load factors). For this we need another algorithm, which was developed by Eisner & Severance (76), and which finds the hull for an m module problem in no more than $m+1$ applications of the network flow algorithm.

Having found the critical load factors for the modules of a program, it becomes very simple to find the optimal assignment for any given load factor f. There is no need to apply the network flow algorithm—one simply goes down the list of critical load factors, comparing each with f and appropriately assigning the corresponding module. No more than m comparisons are required—this permits us to revaluate the optimal assignment very rapidly when the load changes.

As an example, consider the list of critical load factors given in Table 5.1 When the load factor is 0.55, modules 2, 3 and 5 are assigned to P_1 and modules 1, 4 and 6 to P_2. Should the load increase to 0.61,

Table 5.1	
Module	Critical Load Factor
1	0.5
2	0.7
3	0.7
4	0.3
5	0.6
6	0.4

module 5 will move from P_1 to P_2.

5.2. Varying Load on Two Processors

5.2.1. Formulation

Let us now consider the case where load on both processors varies. We will call our two processors X and Y instead of P_1 and P_2. We assume that the load on these two machines is described by the real positive numbers x and y respectively. A specific pair of load levels $<x,y>$ is called a *load point* and may lie anywhere in the positive XY plane.

The cost of running a module A on processor X is assumed to vary linearly with the load on X. The constant of proportionality is denoted a_x. Thus the cost of running module A on processor X is $a_x x$ and, similarly, the cost of running A on Y is $a_y y$*.

The cost of communication between a pair of nodes, should they not be coresident, is assumed to be constant over all possible values of load. At the end of this chapter we will discuss the case where communication cost also varies.

---

*For clarity of presentation, we have assumed that x and y vary from 0 to ∞, thereby implying that at load zero each module executes in zero time. This should create no difficulties in the implementation of this work because load will, in practice, be constrained to lie between some x_{min} and x_{max} and some y_{min} and y_{max}. Thus the shortest time in which a module can execute on processor X would be $a_x x_{min} > 0$.

	Runcost On	Runcost On	Communication Costs				
			Table 5.2				
Module	X	Y	1	2	3	4	5
1	$10x$	$11y$	-	3	7	8	0
2	$2x$	$37y$		-	0	1	0
3	x	$5y$			-	0	7
4	∞	$7y$				-	9
5	$4x$	$4y$					-
	x=load on X	y=load on Y					

Consider the cost figures shown in Table 5.2. Here we have a problem involving 5 modules. The run costs of each module on each processor are given as variables in x and y. The communication costs are for the indicated pair of modules, should they not be coresident. These costs are inserted into the assignment graph of Figure 5.4, as described in Chapter 3. Each cut in this graph corresponds to an assignment and vice versa. The weight of each cut equals the cost of the corresponding assignment. For example, the thick line in Figure 5.4 shows a cut that assigns modules 1 and 2 to processor X and the remaining modules to processor Y. The weight of this cut is given by the equation $z=12x+16y+16$, this being the sum of the weights on the constituent edges. In general, a cut will have weight $z=Mx+Ny+C$, when $M(N)$ equals the sum of run costs of modules assigned to $X(Y)$. C equals the sum of the communication costs between modules that are not coresident.

As in the previous Section, we will identify a cut by listing the set of nodes that it assigns to processor X (the remaining nodes must necessarily be assigned to processor Y). Thus the cut indicated in Figure 5.4 is denoted {1,2}.

We will call the equation of the weight of a cut (or assignment) just the *equation of a cut* (or assignment) for brevity. The *cardinality* of a cut or assignment is the cardinality of (i.e the number of elements in) the set of nodes it assigns to processor X.

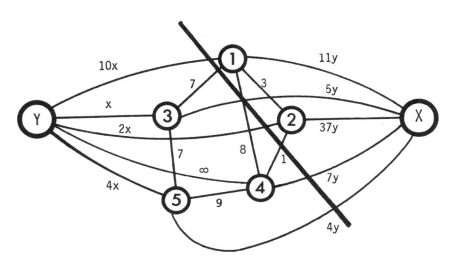

Figure 5.4 Assignment graph for the two-dimensional problem shown in Table 5.2

The assignment that puts no modules on X is called the *Null* assignment, denoted Φ, and has an equation of the form $z=Ny$. The assignment that puts all modules on X is called the *Universal* assignment, denoted U, and has an equation of the form $z=Mx$.

The general equation of a cut $z=Mx+Ny+C$ represents a plane in 3-space. Since there are 2^n possible assignments for a problem involving n modules and two processors, we will have 2^n such equations of planes. The constants M, N and C are all non-negative (because execution and communication costs are all non-negative) and, as a result, none of the planes intersect with the XY plane within the positive quadrant. Every plane has a non-negative intercept with the Z axis (since $C \geq 0$). The slopes of these planes in the X and Y directions are also nonnegative (since M, $N \geq 0$).

We will henceforth call the positive quadrant of the XY plane the *load plane* because each point on it represents a load point. At a given load point $<x,y>$, the lowermost of the 2^n planes (the plane with the smallest z-coordinate) is one that represents the optimal assignment.

This may be found by substituting the specific values of x and y into the assignment graph and applying a network flow algorithm to it, as described in Chapter 3.

As we are interested only in optimal assignments, we need consider only the lowermost plane at each $<x,y>$. A little reflection will reveal that these lowermost planes intersect to form a *convex polyhedron** whose faces correspond to specific assignments. We call this the *assignment polyhedron* because each of its faces represents an assignment that is optimal for all load points $<x,y>$ that lie within its projection on the XY plane. Figure 5.5 shows a typical assignment polyhedron.

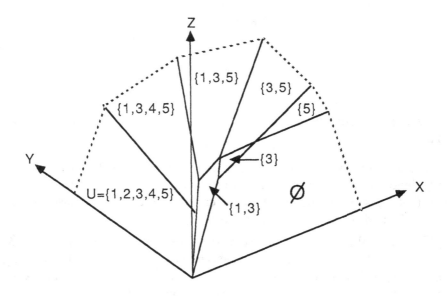

Figure 5.5 Three-dimensional view of an assignment polyhedron for a problem with 5 modules. Dotted boundaries indicate where infinite regions have been truncated.

---

*A polyhedron is a three dimensional solid whose sides or 'faces' are polygons. A polyhedron is convex if a line joining any two points inside it lies wholly inside it.

5.2.2. The Load Plane

The assignment polyhedron described in the previous section is convex. It follows that each individual face is a convex polygon and further that the projection of the polygon onto the XY plane (the load plane) is made up of convex polygons.

The load plane is thus dissected into convex polygonal regions each of which, having been projected by a face, corresponds to an assignment that is optimal for all load points that fall within it, and is labeled accordingly. Figure 5.6 shows the load plane corresponding to the polyhedron of Figure 5.5, which is derived from a graph having eight module nodes.

Stone's Nesting Theorem states that if the load on only machine Y increases the optimal assignment will change such that modules move away from machine Y onto machine X and only in that direction. This

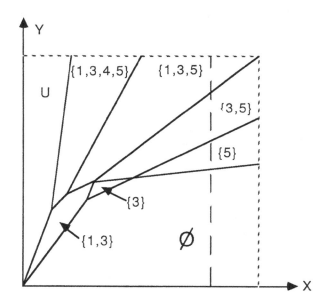

Figure 5.6 The load plane corresponding to the polyhedron of Figure 5.5.

is clear from Figure 5.6 in which the vertical dashed line, parallel to the Y axis, represents an increase in the load on processor Y, while the load on processor X is maintained at a constant value. Traveling in the positive Y direction, we encounter regions Φ, {5}, {3,5}, {1,3,5}. The corresponding property holds if we keep the load on Y constant and vary the load on X.

The load plane has the following properties.

(1) A horizontal or vertical line through the load plane cannot cut through more than $m+1$ regions (m is the number of modules). This follows from the Nesting Theorem.

(2) Each point $<x,y>$ on the load plane falls within a region that represents an assignment that is equal to or contained in the assignment at $<x-\Delta x, y+\Delta y>$, $(\Delta x, \Delta y > 0)$ (Figure 5.7). This also follows from the Nesting Theorem.

(3) The lines defining the regions of the load plane all have positive slope. This follows from property 2 above. A line with negative

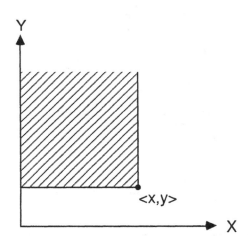

Figure 5.7 Property (2): The assignment at $<x,y>$ must be contained in every assignment in the shaded region.

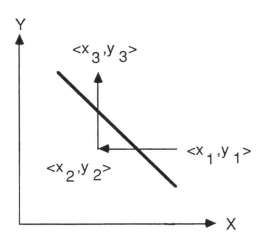

Figure 5.8 Property (3): The line separating two regions cannot have negative slope.

slope cannot separate two regions. For example, in Figure 5.8, suppose $\langle x_1, y_1 \rangle$, $\langle x_3, y_3 \rangle$ are contained in one region and $\langle x_2, y_2 \rangle$ in another, and a line of negative slope separates the two regions. Then the assignment at $\langle x_1, y_1 \rangle$, must be contained in the assignment at $\langle x_2, y_2 \rangle$, which in turn must be contained in $\langle x_3, y_3 \rangle$. This is possible only if all three points belong to the same region. (This property may also be established using arguments based on the convexity of the polyhedron and the properties of the equations of the planes.)

(4) Any continuous or piecewise continuous curve that has negative slope everywhere along its length must pass through successively nested regions (Figure 5.9). Clearly, this curve cannot pass through more than $m+1$ regions.

(5) If we represent each region in the load plane by a node and draw a directed edge between nodes representing adjacent regions in the direction of nesting, we obtain a planar acyclic directed graph. No path in this graph has length greater than $m+1$.

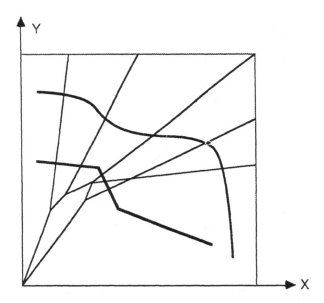

Figure 5.9 Property (4): Any curve that has negative slope throughout its length cannot pass through more than $m+1$ regions.

(6) The X axis can be touched only by the Φ region for all $x>0$. This is because the equation for the Φ region is $z=Ny$ which is zero for all $y=0$ and all other regions have $z>0$ for $y>0$. Similarly, the Y axis can be touched only by the U region, for all $y>0$.

(7) The regions for very large values of x and y are all unbounded. These 'fringe' regions include the Φ and U regions.

5.2.3. Finding the Load Plane

In the problem of Section 5.1, where the load on only one processor varied, the number of line segments on the convex hull of optimal assignments (Figure 5.3) was equal to the number of modules, m. For the present problem, the analogous quantity is the number of faces on the assignment polyhedron (Figure 5.5) or, equivalently, the number of regions on the load plane (Figure 5.6). This number is not bounded by m or even a polynomial in m. Assignment graphs whose load planes

have an exponential number of regions have been constructed by Carstensen (83). These carefully constructed graphs represent worst cases
which are unlikely to be encountered in practice. It is the author's
experience that the number of faces on a polyhedron generated from an
m module graph with random weights will usually lie between m and
m^2.

Gusfield (83) has solved the problem of finding all the regions in
the load plane. The time required by this algorithm varies with the
number of line segments (i.e. sides of regions) on the load plane. It can
find the entire load plane in time $O(m^6)$ per line segment.

5.2.4. Critical Load Lines

Given the load plane, we obviously need some means for utilizing
it in our assignment problem. In this section we present an efficient
technique for finding the assignment of all modules of the program,
given the load point.

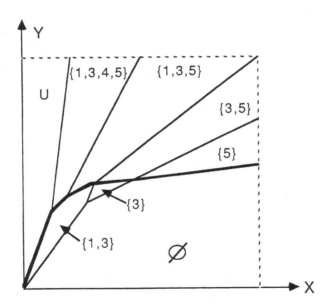

Figure 5.10 Critical load line for module 3.

Let us examine the load plane shown in Figure 5.10, concentrating our attention on module 5. We observe that the load plane may be divided into two super regions such that if the load point is in one region, module 5 is assigned to processor X and if in the other, it is assigned to processor Y. In Figure 5.10, the super region comprising regions {5}, {3,5}, {1,3,5}, {1,3,4,5}, and U is the one for which module 5 is assigned to processor X. Clearly, one such division of the load plane exists for each module. This leads to the following concept.

Definition. The *critical load line* for a module is a piecewise continuous line on the load plane, such that if the load point falls to the right of (or below) this line, the optimal assignment will place that module on processor Y. If the load point falls to the left of (or above) this line, the module is assigned to processor X by the optimal assignment.

The thick line shown in Figure 5.10 is the critical load line for module 5.

The following properties of critical load lines may be enumerated.

(1) A critical load line starts at the origin and continues indefinitely.

(2) Each segment of a critical load line is a straight line with positive slope. (Negative slopes would violate the nesting property.)

(3) The y coordinate of the critical load line increases monotonically with the x coordinate (follows from property 2 above).

(4) At least two critical load lines pass through the point of intersection of three regions on the load plane (Figure 5.11). This point of intersection is, in fact, a vertex of the assignment polyhedron.

(5) The set of m critical load lines, one for each module, completely specifies the load plane. If the z coordinate is included at each breakpoint of each critical load line, then the set of critical load lines completely specifies the assignment polyhedron.

The critical load line associated with a particular module may be used to find the optimal assignment for that module for a given load point. Suppose we are given a critical load line (Figure 5.12) specified by the end points of its segments. We may determine whether a load point $<x_1,y_1>$ lies above or below this point as follows.

(1) Divide the load plane into vertical strips determined by the end points of the segments of the critical load line.

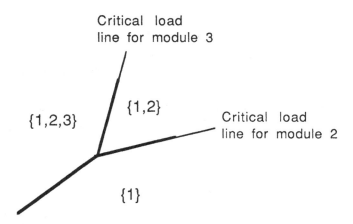

Figure 5.11 At least two critical load lines pass through a point of intersection of three regions.

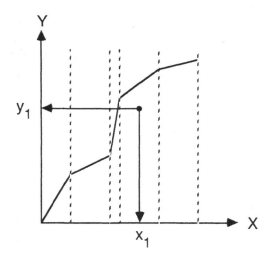

Figure 5.12 Determining whether a point $\langle x_1, y_1 \rangle$ lies above or below a given critical load line. f denotes the load on processor 1.

(2) Determine which strip the x coordinate of the point $\langle x_1, y_1 \rangle$ lies in. Since the y coordinate of a critical load line increases monotonically

with x (property (3) above), we may use a binary search at this step.

(3) Determine whether the y coordinate lies above or below the segment within the strip found in step 2.

The search in step 2 takes $O(\log L)$ time, where L is the number of line segments in the critical load line. Step 3 takes constant time. The determination of the optimal assignment for all m modules will thus take $O(m\log L_{max})$ time, where L_{max} is the maximum number of line segments in any critical load line.

5.3. Varying Communication Costs

The results of the previous sections can be extended to include the case of varying communication costs. Here, in addition to the execution costs being multiplied by loads x and y, as shown in Figure 5.4, the communication costs are multiplied by the communication load z. Each cut now has weight $w=Mx+Ny+Cz$, where M and N are the sums of the execution costs on processors X and Y, as before. C is the sum of all intermodule communication costs for non-coresident modules and z represents the load on the communication link. In practice, the increase in communication costs would be due to congestion on the interprocessor communication link caused by jobs or applications other than our own distributed program.

If we fix the value of z at any constant, this problem reduces to the two-dimensional problem of Section 5.2 and we can use Gusfield's algorithm to find the load plane. Figure 5.13 sketches a load plane at a fixed value of z. Before proceeding further, it is important to clarify the difference between this figure and Figure 5.5.

In both figures the x and y axes represent load on the two processors. In figure 5.5 the z axis represents the cost of an assignment and the object shown is an assignment polyhedron. In Figure 5.13, on the other hand, the z axis represents the load on the communication link. This figure shows a 3-dimensional volume, each point of which represents a load point. We call this volume the *load space*.

As discussed above, the weight of a cut in an assignment graph representing a problem with varying communication costs is of the form $w=Mx+Ny+Cz$. This results in an important property.

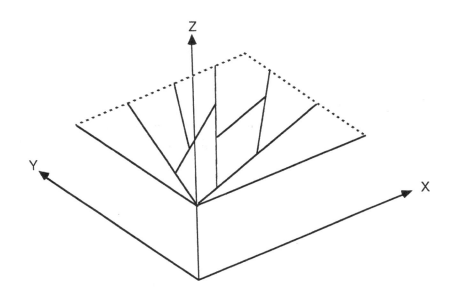

Figure 5.13 A load plane at a fixed value of z.

(1) If a cut is optimal at a specific load point $\langle x_1, y_1, z_1 \rangle$ it will remain optimal at every load point $\langle ax_1, ay_1, az_1 \rangle$, where a is a positive constant.

To appreciate this, consider two cuts with equations $w_1 = M_1 x + N_1 y + C_1 z$ and $w_2 = M_2 x + N_2 y + C_2 z$. If $w_1 < w_2$ at some $\langle x_1, y_1, z_1 \rangle$ then $w_1/w_2 = (M_1 x_1 + N_1 y_1 + C_1 z_1)/(M_2 x_1 + N_2 y_1 + C_2 z_1) < 1$. This ratio will remain unchanged if we multiply each of x_1, y_1 and z_1 with some constant a. Given a fixed point $\langle x_1, y_1, z_1 \rangle$, the set of points $\langle ax_1, ay_1, az_1 \rangle$ form a line passing through the origin and $\langle x_1, y_1, z_1 \rangle$. When $a=0$ this line is at the origin; when $a=1$ it is at $\langle x_1, y_1, z_1 \rangle$. It follows that

(2) if we fix $z=z_1$, obtain the load plane and find a certain cut to be optimal over some region in this load plane, then this cut will also be optimal in any other load plane obtained by setting $z=z_2$.

This is illustrated in Figure 5.14 where we can see that if a cut is optimal somewhere in one load plane, it must be optimal somewhere in every other load plane. In fact the two load planes at two distinct values of z are distorted copies of each other. This figure also illustrates that

(3) the volume enclosed by the lines passing through the origin and all points on the perimeter of a region on a specific load plane includes precisely those points for which the cut represented by the region is optimal.

In Section 5.2 we considered the case where the load on only the two processors varied, and saw that a two dimensional load plane could specify all optimal assignments for all possible values of load. There

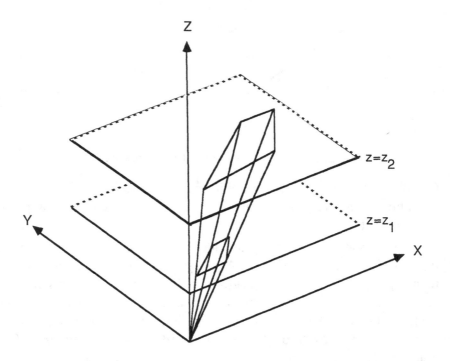

Figure 5.14 If a cut is optimal in one load plane, it must be optimal somewhere in every other load plane. Cuts are optimal over cones that have convex polygonal cross sections and apexes at the origin.

was a convex polygonal region corresponding to each optimal assignment. For the present problem, we have varying load on two processors and on the communication link. Here the portion of three-dimensional space for which $x,y,z>0$ (the load space) represents every possible combination of loads. The volume defined by property 3 above represents those points for which a specific assignment is optimal. The load space is partitioned into a number of cones which have a common apex at the origin, have a convex polygonal cross-section and extend indefinitely (Figure 5.14).

To find all the cones in the load space we need only find one load plane at a convenient value of z and then draw lines from the origin through every vertex of each region in this load plane. There is in fact no need to actually construct the cones for the purpose of finding the optimal assignment. Given that we have constructed a load plane for some $z=z_1$ using Gusfield's algorithm, the optimal assignment at any $\langle x_2,y_2,z_2 \rangle$ can be found as follows.

(1) Draw a line from the origin through $\langle x_2,y_2,z_2 \rangle$

(2) Compute the point $\langle x_1,y_1 \rangle$ where this line passes through the plane $z=z_1$.

(3) Apply the search procedure of Section 5.2.4 to find the optimal assignment for $\langle x_1,y_1 \rangle$ on the load plane $z=z_1$. This optimal assignment will also be optimal for the load point $\langle x_2,y_2,z_2 \rangle$ as illustrated in Figure 5.15.

The operations in step 1 and 2 of this procedure take constant time, that is time independent of the size of the problem. Step 3 is exactly the procedure of Section 5.2.4 and thus takes time $O(m\log L_{max})$ where L_{max} is the maximum number of segments in any load line.

The discussion in this section assumes that the cost of executing a module $A(B)$ on processor $X(Y)$ is equal to $a_x x(b_y y)$ where $x(y)$ is a real, positive number that represents the load on processor $X(Y)$ and $a_x(b_y)$ are constants of proportionality. Similarly, the cost of intermodule communications between modules X and Y, should they not be coresident is $c_{xy} z$ where z represents the load on the communication link. All cost functions pass through the origin (i.e. they are zero when load is zero). This is why the regions of optimality are cone shaped.

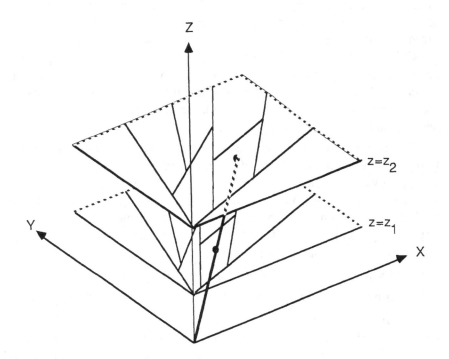

Figure 5.15 If the load plane at $z=z_1$ is known, the optimal assignment at any point $\langle x_2, y_2, z_2 \rangle$ can be found.

When the cost functions do not have the form described above, regions of optimality will not be cone shaped and the techniques of this section will not apply. The question of whether techniques exist for efficient assignment under varying load conditions for more general cost functions is open.

5.4. Summary

In multiple computer systems, the optimal assignment of a distributed program is sensitive to load conditions on the processors and on the traffic on the interprocessor communication link. We have discussed this problem for the case of dual processor systems and shown how all optimal assignments can be computed and stored in advance.

Once this has been done, the optimal assignment for any given load condition can be found very quickly.

When the load on only one processor varies, it can be proved that there are no more than $m+1$ different assignments for a problem with m modules. When the load on both processors varies, there is no polynomial bound on the number of different assignments in the worst case. However, the number of assignments encountered in practice is usually small. The number of different assignments remains unchanged if the load on the communication links is also allowed to vary.

In addition to providing a means for adjusting assignments very rapidly when the load conditions in a system change, the results in this chapter also permit us to find optimal *global* assignments of several programs, as will be discussed in the following Chapter.

CHAPTER 6
The Sum-Bottleneck Path Algorithm

In the preceding three chapters we have seen how maximum flow and shortest path algorithms can be used to find the optimal assignment of a serial distributed program. Recent research has shown that a *sum-bottleneck path algorithm* can be employed to find the optimal assignment of the modules of a parallel or pipelined program in several types of distributed systems. This approach can also be used to find the optimal *global assignment* of a set of independent serial distributed programs over a single-host, multiple-satellite system. Since this technique can explicitly take concurrency into account, it represents a major development over the work presented in the preceding chapters.

6.1. Motivations

We have seen in the previous three chapters that network flow and shortest path algorithms can be used to solve the problem of optimally assigning the modules of a distributed program over a multiple computer system. The techniques presented in these chapters can be used to minimize the time required to execute a program if the program is serial. That is, even though there are many modules and several processors, only one module is active on one processor at one time.

The problem of optimally assigning the modules of a parallel program has remained open. In its most general form, this problem can be shown to belong to the notorious NP-complete class of problems for which no efficient algorithms are known. In the present chapter we report very recent research (Bokhari 87) in which it has been established that if the structures of the program and of the multiple computer system are restricted in certain ways, this problem can indeed be solved efficiently.

At the heart of this chapter is the notion of Sum-Bottleneck paths, which is described in the following section. An algorithm that finds the optimal Sum-Bottleneck path can be used to solve the problem of assigning a chain-like parallel or pipelined program over a chain-connected multicomputer system, as discussed in Section 6.3. In Section 6.4 we show that this algorithm can also be used to find the optimal global assignment of several chain-like parallel programs in a single-host, multiple-satellite system.

The major result of this chapter is the algorithm for finding the optimal global assignment of multiple serial programs in a single-host multiple satellite system (Section 6.5). This algorithm combines the results of the previous three chapters and is likely to be of considerable practical relevance. Finally, in Section 6.6 we show how a tree-structured parallel program can be partitioned in a single-host multiple satellite system.

6.2. Definitions

In Chapter 2, we defined a *weighted graph* to be one in which there is a real number associated with each edge. We also discussed the notion of the *weight* of a path in a weighted graph. This is the *sum* of the weights on all the constituent edges in the path. The *bottleneck weight* of a path was defined as the weight of the *heaviest* edge in the path.

We now introduce the concept of a *doubly weighted graph*. This a graph in which there are *two* weights associated with each edge e: the *Sum Weight* $\sigma(e)$ and the *Bottleneck Weight* $\beta(e)$. Thus, instead of a single weight on each edge, as in the ordinary weighted graph, we have an ordered pair of weights one each edge.

Consider a path in this graph that is composed of a sequence of edges e_1, e_2, e_3, $\cdots$. The Sum Weight of this path, S, is the *sum* of the weights of all $\sigma(e_i)$. The Bottleneck Weight of the path, B, is the *largest* of all $\beta(e_i)$. These definitions are the same as those stated separately in Chapter 2, for ordinary weighted graphs.

The *Sum-Bottleneck weight* of a path in a doubly weighted graph is defined to be max(S,B), i.e., the *larger* of the two types of weights, and is called *SB weight* for brevity. The *optimal Sum-Bottleneck path* (briefly, *optimal SB path*) between two nodes in a doubly weighted

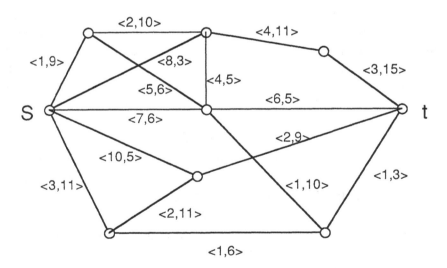

Figure 6.1 A doubly weighted graph. The optimal path between nodes *s* and *t* has weight 10.

graph is the path for which the Sum-Bottleneck weight is *minimum*. In Figure 6.1, the labels on each edge represent $<\sigma,\beta>$; the optimal SB path between nodes s and t has weight 10.

Lawler (76) has previously used doubly weighted graphs for certain combinatorial optimization problems. The specific interpretation of the weights as sum and bottleneck, and the application of this concept to partitioning problems is due to Bokhari (87), who also presents an efficient algorithm for finding the optimal SB path. This algorithm has $O(n^2\log e)$ complexity, for a graph with n nodes and e edges.

The optimal SB path in a doubly weighted graph in which all β weights are zero corresponds to an ordinary shortest path and can be found using Dijkstra's algorithm in $O(n^2)$ time. Similarly, when all the σ weights are zero, it corresponds to an ordinary minimum bottleneck weight path, which can be found using a variant of Dijkstra's algorithm in $O(n^2)$ time (Edmonds & Karp 72).

6.3. Partitioning Chains over Chains

We first describe how the standard minimum bottleneck path algorithm can be used to partition chain-structured programs over a chain-connected computer system. A chain structured program has m modules numbered $1 \cdots m$ and has an interconnection pattern such that module i is connected only to modules $i+1$ and $i-1$ (excluding, of course, modules 1 and m, which are connected only to modules 2 and $m-1$ respectively).

We work under the constraint that each processor have a contiguous subchain of modules assigned to it. That is, partitions of the chains have to be such that module i and $i+1$ are assigned to the same or to adjacent processors. We call this the *contiguity* constraint.

Chain-like program graphs arise in many applications, most notably signal processing and image analysis. In these applications speedup of program execution is obtained by *pipelining* operations, much like an automobile assembly line. We will start by describing three environments where this problem arises, and then show how an assignment graph is constructed in which an optimal bottleneck path corresponds to the optimal assignment. We will also describe how memory constraints can be taken into account.

6.3.1. Signal Processing

A common requirement in signal processing systems is to repeatedly apply a fixed sequence of operations (or transforms) to an essentially unending series of signals. For example, each arriving packet or frame of data may have to be Fourier transformed, multiplied by a fixed frequency, filtered, etc. This kind of computing has a serial or chain-like structure and naturally lends itself to pipelining (Bolch et al. 83).

On a uniprocessor, the maximum rate at which we can process incoming data frames is determined by the time required for the processor to apply all the required steps to one frame. This computation can easily be pipelined by putting each process on a separate processor. Since the communication pattern of the processes is serial, the processors need only be connected in a chain. The maximum rate of processing is determined by the processor that takes the longest amount of time to perform its task (the *bottleneck* processor). This is an expensive solution in that it requires as many processors as processes. It may also be extremely inefficient because many processors may be very lightly loaded and spend most of their time waiting for the bottleneck processor

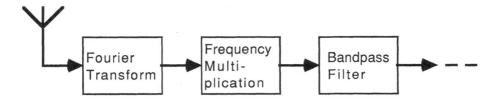

Figure 6.2 Typical processing steps in a communication system.

to finish its work.

The following problem can thus be identified. Given a set of m modules connected in a chain-like fashion and a chain-connected multiprocessor system of size $n<m$, find the assignment of modules to processors that minimizes the load on the most heavily loaded processor. The contiguity constraint ensures that two modules that communicate lie on directly connected processors.

The optimal assignment of subchains to processors is influenced by

(1) the time required to run each module on one frame of data (which may vary across processors, in case they are dissimilar),

(2) the amount of intermodule communication (which may be non-uniform because once a frame has been transformed, it may have a different number of data points), and

(3) the speeds of the links between pairs of connected processors.

6.3.2. Image Analysis

Similar problems arise in the field of image analysis, where the requirement is to take an image or set of images and to apply various operators to it (Sternberg 83). In this application the possibility exists

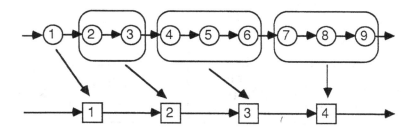

Figure 6.3 A nine module chain mapped onto a four processor chain.

of obtaining a degree of pipelining greater than the number of different types of operations to be performed. For example, if one needs to apply an operator to every 3×3 square of pixels in the image, it is possible to have as many pipelined stages as there are 3×3 squares in the image. This assumes that frames can be forwarded from processor to processor at a sufficiently high rate.

6.3.3. Partial Differential Equations

A straightforward technique for the parallel solution of certain types of partial differential equations on a non-uniform mesh is to partition the domain into vertical strips. An estimate is made of the values within a strip during each iteration. The time required to process each strip is dependent on the density of the mesh in it. Since strips only influence adjacent strips, the communication pattern of this problem is also chain like and it can be executed in parallel on a chain-connected system (Saltz 85). There again emerges the problem of the optimal assignment of a chain of modules (in this case strips of the domain) over a chain of processors.

The structure of the problem is the same as that shown in Figure 6.2, except that the edges interconnecting communicating modules or processors are undirected (communications take place in both directions). The time required to complete one step of the computation is equal to the time required by the most heavily loaded processor to complete that one step. The important difference between this case and the signal or image processing examples described above is that this is *parallel* not pipelined processing. As we will see in the following sections, the assignment algorithm is insensitive to this difference.

6.3.4. Execution and Communication Costs

For the case of pipelined processing, the time required for a processor to finish executing the work assigned to it is equal to the sum of the times to execute all of the modules that reside on it. A communication overhead is added to this sum to account for the time taken to transmit the result from one processor to the next.

In Figure 6.3, for example, the execution time for processor 3 is the time required for processor 3 to execute modules 4, 5 and 6 on a frame of data. The communication time is the time to transmit information from module 3 in processor 6 to module 7 in processor 4. As in earlier

Chapters, the time required to communicate between modules when they are resident on the same processor is assumed to be negligible. If need be, a non-negligible intraprocessor communication time can be accounted for by lumping it with the execution times of the modules.

Since this is pipelined processing, during the time that processor 3 applies modules 4, 5 and 6 to frame i, processor 2 applies modules 2 and 3 to frame $i+1$ and so on. The time for all processors to finish processing one frame of information each is determined by the most heavily loaded (i.e. bottleneck) processor.

In the case of parallel processing, costs are added up in exactly the same fashion. However, in this case, execution and intermodule communication need not occur in well defined phases—they may be distributed all over the lifetime of the program. At any one point in time, all processors work on different parts of the same problem unlike the pipelined case where each processor works on a distinct frame of data. Interprocessor communication in the parallel processing case is bidirectional as processors need to interchange information.

We assume that we are dealing with "production" programs, that is programs that execute repeatedly so that their behavior is well understood and for which the costs of communication and execution can be measured accurately.

6.3.5. Construction of Assignment Graph

We first draw up a layered graph that contains all information about the execution and communication times of the modules. A path in this graph corresponds to the assignment of modules to processors. The weight of the heaviest edge in any path corresponds to the time required to execute the assignment in parallel or pipelined fashion. Thus, having drawn up the graph, all we have to do is to find the *minimum bottleneck path*.

In Figure 6.4, each layer corresponds to a processor and the label on each node corresponds to a subchain of modules. Any path connecting nodes s and t corresponds to the assignment of a subchain of modules to processors. For example, the thick edges correspond to the assignment of Figure 6.3. Many edges have been omitted in Figure 6.4 to avoid a congested diagram.

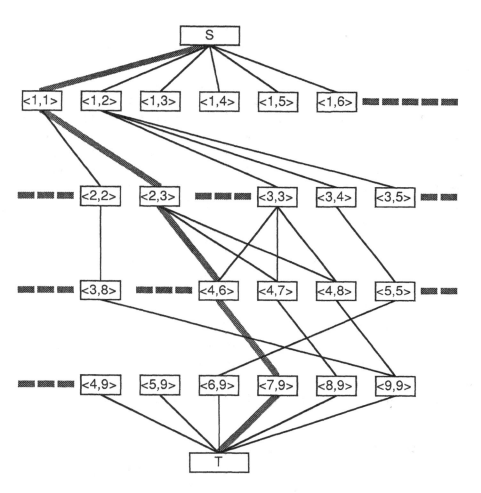

Figure 6.4 A layered graph for a problem with 9 modules and 4 processors.

This graph is generated according to the following rules. Each layer contains all subchains of nodes, in other words all pairs $<i,j>$ such that $1 \leq i \leq j \leq m$. A node labeled $<i,j>$ is connected to all nodes $<j+1,k>$, in the layer below it for all j except 1 and n. All nodes $<i,j>$ $(<i,m>)$ in the first (last) layer are connected to node s (t). As stated above, each path from s to t represents an assignment of subchains to processors under the contiguity constraint. If this path contains node $<i,j>$ of layer k, this represents the assignment of modules i through j to processor k. There is a path from s to t corresponding to every possible contiguous assignment and vice versa.

Weights are added to the edges of this layered graph as follows. In layer k, each edge emanating downwards from node $<i,j>$ is first weighted with the time required for processor k to process node i through j. This accounts for the computation time. The communication time is now included in the graph: to the weight on the edge joining node $<a,b>$ in layer k to node $<b+1,d>$ in layer $k+1$ is added the time to communicate between module b and $b+1$ over the link connecting processors k and $k+1$. It is clear that the influence of both the amount of data transmitted between modules b and $b+1$ as well as the speed of the link between processors k and $k+1$ can be included in the graph.

To account for memory constraints on individual processors, we add up the memory requirements of all modules in all subchains. If the sum for nodes i through j exceeds the capacity of processor k, node $<i,j>$ in layer k is deleted, along with all edges incident on it.

6.3.6. Finding the Optimal Assignment

The minimum weight bottleneck path can be found using a variant of Dijkstra's algorithm in time proportional to the square of the number of nodes in the graph. However, the layered structure of the graph permits us to find the path even more efficiently. This is done using a simple labeling procedure, described by Bokhari (87), in $O(m^3n)$ time.

6.4. Partitioning Multiple Chains in a Host-Satellite System

The optimal SB path algorithm finds an application in the Host-Satellite system of Figure 6.5. This Figure shows a large host computer connected to several satellites which receive data from a real-time environment (for example, an aircraft). The data streams entering each satellite have to be processed in a pipelined fashion (as in Figure 6.1). The individual satellites may have different computational capabilities, the data streams could have different arrival rates (in frames per second), and the processing steps performed on each stream need not be identical.

The program running on each relatively small satellite can be partitioned between the satellite and the larger, more powerful, host to improve processing time. However, in moving modules to the host we adversely impact the performance of other satellites. The complex

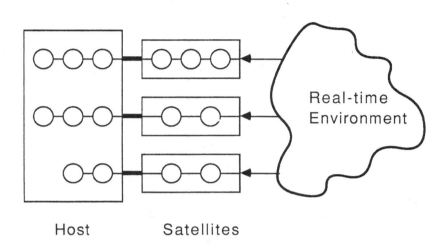

Figure 6.5 A Host-Satellite System processing real-time data.

interactions between the loads of the satellites via the shared host make this a difficult problem.

The factors influencing the cost of an assignment for this problem are the same as those enumerated in Section 6.3, except that now there is a different set of costs for each satellite. We have for each module i of satellite j, the time required to run it on the satellite, e_{ij}, and on the host, h_{ij}. For each pair of modules i and $i+1$ from satellite j we have the time required for interprocessor communications, c_{ij}, should i be assigned to the host and $i+1$ to the satellite.

Since all processing is done in a pipelined fashion, the times for execution and communication are the times to process one frame of data. Our assignment should be such that the time required to process one frame each from *all* streams is minimized. It is assumed that all data streams are to be treated equally. Should we wish to give some data streams more importance than others, we can scale the costs appropriately. For example, to process 5 frames of stream 1 for every 3 frames of stream 2 we can multiply the cost figures of streams 1 and 2 by 5 and 3 respectively.

For simplicity, we will assume that all chains have precisely m modules each and that there are n satellites. Modules are numbered from left to right. The partition point of each chain is defined by the highest numbered module from the chain that is assigned to the host. For a given partition of the n chains between the host and the n satellites, the time required by the entire system to complete the processing of one frame of data from each stream is determined by the greater of (1) the individual load on the most heavily loaded satellite and (2) the sum of the collective load on the host.

From among the satellites, the one which is most heavily loaded—the bottleneck satellite—determines the processing time. The time taken by the host, on the other hand, is determined by the *sum* of all the loads on it. The greater of these two is the actual time since either the host waits for the slowest satellite to finish, or vice versa.

6.4.1. Construction of the Assignment Graph

All information related to this problem can be captured in a new kind of assignment graph shown in Figure 6.6. This graph has n layers, one for each of the satellites. Each layer has m nodes, one for each module. An edge extends from each node in layer k to all nodes in layer $k+1$. There is a start node s above the first layer and a terminating node t after the last layer.

The assignment graph in Figure 6.6 is for a problem with 5 satellites, with 5 modules on each satellite. There is a one-to-one correspondence between paths from s to t and partitionings of the 5 chains between host and satellites. Thick edges in this figure represent the assignment of module 1-4 of chain 1, 1 of chain 2, 1-3 of chain 3 etc. to the host and the remaining nodes of each chain to their respective satellite.

Double edge weights in this graph represent run times. Each edge leaving node j in layer k is first given a σ weight equal to the cost of the sum of execution times of module 1 through j of chain k. The β weight of this edge is the sum of execution times of modules $j+1$ through m of chain k. To *both* these weights is added the communication cost for modules j and $j+1$ over the link connecting the host to the satellite k (this is because the communication overhead is incurred on both sides of the link). Edges extending out of node s have zero weight.

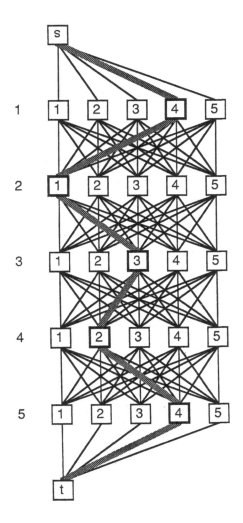

Figure 6.6 Assignment Graph for Host-Satellite Problem.

6.4.2. Solution

The SB weight of any s to t path in this graph corresponds to the time required by the corresponding assignment. The optimal SB path, which corresponds to the best assignment may be found using the optimal SB path algorithm described in (Bokhari 87). As in Section 6.3, the layered structure of the graph results in substantial savings in running time. For a problem with n satellites and m modules, the assignment graph has $O(m^2n)$ edges. The SB path algorithm thus takes

$O(m^2 n \log m)$ time, assuming $m > n$.

6.5. Global Assignments in Multiple-Satellite System

In Section 3.1 we described Stone's solution to the problem of partitioning a serial program in a single-host, single-satellite system. Section 5.1 described Stone's analysis of the behavior of the optimal assignments as a function of the load on the host. The analysis of Section 5.1 assumes that the host is time-shared so that, in addition to executing some of the modules of the distributed program, it also has to serve a number of other unrelated programs. We have no control over the load on the host caused by these unrelated programs and can only adjust the assignment of our single distributed program in order to minimize its execution time.

We now consider a single-host, *multiple*-satellite system, similar to the one discussed in Section 6.4, but one in which each satellite executes a serial modular program with an arbitrary interconnection structure (Figure 6.7). For an n satellite system, there will be n separate programs. These could all be copies of one common program, could be all unique, or could be some combination of the two. The satellites may have dissimilar capabilities. Some modules from each of the satellites can be placed on the host to take advantage of the host's greater power. However, when several satellites assign some of their modules to the host, the host's effective power goes down. As a consequence, the time required by all satellites to finish running their programs increases. We are faced with the problem of finding the optimal *global* assignment, i.e. specifying which modules from each satellite are to be assigned to the host so that the time required by all satellites to finish their work is minimized.

Many distributed systems in the real world are in the form of a large central host machine with powerful computational and database capabilities connected to a number of small satellites. The satellites run ordinary serial programs and access shared data on the host from time to time. In such environments it can often be worthwhile to partition each satellite's program so that some of its modules run on the host. In order to equitably apportion the host's resources among the several satellites, the global assignment should be such that the time required for the slowest satellite to finish its processing is minimized.

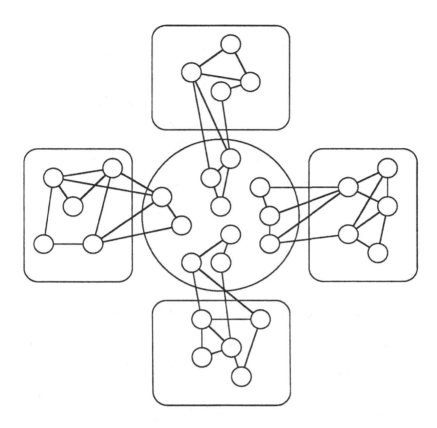

Figure 6.7 A single-host, multiple-satellite system executing arbitrarily structured programs.

In Section 6.4 we showed how multiple independent chains could be partitioned across a host-satellite system so as to minimize the time for execution for the most heavily loaded satellite. The chains could be streams of pipelined signal processing tasks or parallel programs with a chain-like interconnection, as discussed in Section 6.3.

Earlier, in Section 5.1 we discussed Stone's Nesting Theorem which states that when the load on the host increases in a single-host, single-satellite system, modules move away from the host and onto the satellite. Optimal assignments at successively increasing values of load on the host are nested, as illustrated in Figure 6.8.

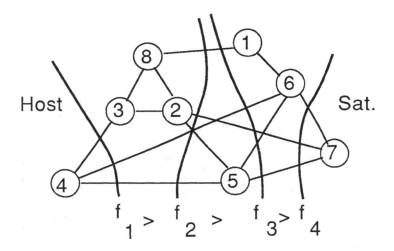

Figure 6.8 Four cuts at successively increasing values of load on the host. Each cut is labeled with the load factor f_i for which it is optimal.

We will now show that the Nesting Theorem allows us to *view* the interconnection of the modules as chain-like, regardless of the actual interconnection. This permits us to solve the problem of optimally assigning or partitioning multiple distributed programs across a single-host, multiple-satellite system, using the SB path algorithm.

6.5.1. Transformation into Chains

As far as the behavior of the optimal assignment under varying load on the host is concerned, the information in Figure 6.8 can be represented by the *loading chain* of Figure 6.9. All program modules lying between two adjacent cuts in Figure 6.8 are lumped together into one super node in Figure 6.9. In this example, the critical load factor property states that if the load on the host is less than f_1, modules 2, 3 and 8 will lie on the host. If the load is more than f_1, they will lie on the satellite. As the load varies, these modules move as a group or clump—there is no value of load for which this group is split up. While this clumping has been observed in real distributed programs (Michel & van Dam 76), it is always possible to contrive execution and communication costs such that no clumping occurs. That is, a program

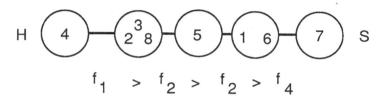

Figure 6.9 Loading chain for the problem of Figure 6.8. Each node represents a cluster of modules.

with m modules gives rise to a loading chain with m nodes. We will assume this worst case in subsequent analysis. It is convenient to renumber the modules of the loading chain in a left to right order.

6.5.2. Construction of the Assignment Graph

Let us suppose that we have a single host connected to n independent satellites. Each of the satellites has an arbitrarily connected serial program of m modules running on it. (To make our discussion easier, we have assumed that each program is composed of the same *number* of modules.)

We assume that each program goes through an unending series of iterations. The number of time units per iteration that the program i spends in module j, should this module be assigned to the host (satellite). is given by h_{ij} (s_{ij}).

For each pair of modules i and j. the interprocessor communication cost c_{ij} is the number of time units per iteration spent in communication between the modules, should they not be coresident.

The loading chains for each separate host-satellite combination can be found using the algorithm of Eisner and Severance (76) as discussed in Section 5.1.3. This takes $O(m^4n)$ time and yields n loading chains of size no more than m each. An assignment of modules in the loading chain can be specified by naming a "pivotal" module p such that nodes $1 \cdots p$ are assigned to the host and $p+1 \cdots m$ to the satellite. We can therefore compute for each node p of the ith loading chain:

(1) Ψ_p, the number of time units of satellite time that it requires per iteration. $\Psi_p = \sum_{j=p+1}^{m} s_{ij}$, i.e. the sum of the individual s_{ij}'s of the modules assigned to the satellite.

(2) H_p, the number of time units of host time that it requires per iteration. $H_p = \sum_{j=1}^{p} s_{ij}$, i.e. the sum of the individual h_{ij}'s of the modules assigned to the host.

(3) C_p, the number of time units of interprocessor communication time that it requires. $C_p = \sum_{i \leq p, j > p} c_{ij}$, i.e. the sum of communication costs between all pairs of modules i, j that are not coresident.

The global assignment of modules from n programs in this system is given by the vector $\pi[i], i=1, n$. Here $\pi[i]$ is the pivotal module defining the assignment of modules in program i. The time required by an assignment is

$$\max(\sum_{i=1}^{n} \{H_\pi[i] + C_\pi[i]\}, \max_{i=1,n}\{\Psi_\pi[i] + H_\pi[i] + C_\pi[i]\}).$$

Let us examine this expression. For a given $\pi[i]$ the sums $\Psi_\pi[i] + H_\pi[i] + C_\pi[i]$ represent the times for the n individual assignments as if the n programs were running on n isolated host-satellite systems. The time for every program to complete one iteration each on the single host system is determined by the slowest, hence the selection of the maximum of these. The time for the host to complete its share of the work is the sum of all $H_\pi[i] + C_\pi[i]$. The time for the entire system to complete one iteration of every program is the maximum of these two quantities.

These times can be used to create a doubly weighted layered graph similar to the one in Figure 6.7. Each layer in this graph corresponds to a loading chain. Each path from s to t corresponds to a $\pi[i]$. All possible $\pi[i]$'s exist in this graph. An edge emanating downward from node p in layer k is given σ weight equal to $H_p + C_p$ and β weight equal to $\Psi_p + H_p + C_p$. The SB weight of each path equals the time required for the corresponding global assignment. The optimal global assignment can be found using the optimal SB path algorithm in $O(m^2 n \log m)$. Thus the time required to solve the overall problem is dominated by the time required to find the individual loading chains i.e. $O(m^4 n)$.

6.6. Partitioning Trees in a Host-Satellite System

We now address the problem of optimally assigning a tree-structured parallel or pipelined program over a single-host, multiple-satellite system in which the satellites are similar. This problem can arise in many industrial process control or monitoring systems where information from many sources is collected by small satellite computers and transmitted to a central host for processing. The processing in such systems is tree-like, with information being input to the leaves of the tree which then process and pass the information up to their parents.

In such systems it is useful if the satellites can perform part of the processing instead of merely collecting and forwarding information. By offloading work to the satellites, we can reduce the load on the host and thus improve the response time of the system. The amount of work that can be assigned to the satellites is constrained by their lower computational power and small memories. The amount of interprocessor communication, which depends on the amount of data being transmitted and the speed of the links, also has to be taken into account when making the assignments.

The solution we present yields the partition that optimizes *pipelined* or *parallel* execution time under the constraint that the root of the tree is always assigned to the host. The remaining nodes may be assigned to the host or to the satellites provided only *maximal subtrees* are assigned to satellites. A maximal subtree is the entire subtree that is separated from the program tree by the deletion of a single edge.

Figure 6.10 shows a 13 node tree that has been partitioned under these constraints. It is assumed that there are as many satellites as leaf nodes in the tree and that we may choose not to use them if the optimal assignment so dictates.

6.6.1. Construction of the Assignment Graph

An assignment graph for this problem is shown in Figure 6.11. This graph is obtained by placing a dummy node Δ below the tree and

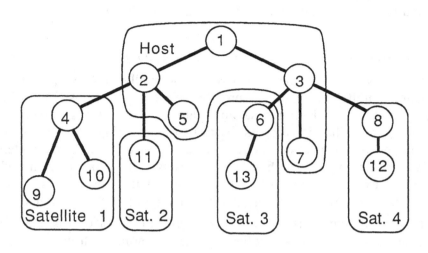

Figure 6.10 A tree structured program partitioned over a host-satellite system.

connecting it to all the leaf nodes. This creates a planar* graph with several regions or faces. The assignment graph is a *directed dual graph*† of this planar graph constructed by placing a node in each region and one node each on the left and right hand sides. These nodes are indicated by squares in Figure 6.11. There is an unambiguous left to right ordering of these nodes (indicated by the sequence $A, B, \cdots, H$ in Figure 6.11). A directed edge is drawn between every pair of nodes that belong to regions that have a common edge. The direction of the edge is from the lower ordered node to the higher. We have omitted the arrowheads in Figure 6.11 since their direction is evident from the node labels.

---

*A planar graph is one which can be drawn on the plane without any edges crossing

†The dual graph D of a planar graph P has one node for every region of P, one region for every node of P and one edge for every edge of P. It is obtained using the procedure described above (Deo 74).

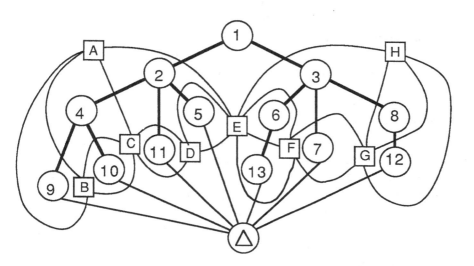

Figure 6.11 The assignment graph for the problem of Figure 6.10.

Each directed path between A and H in the assignment graph corresponds to an assignment of modules over the host satellite system. We assume that we have available for each module i the time required to execute it on the host, h_i and on a satellite, s_i (recall that all satellites are similar in this case). For each edge in the tree connecting parent node i to child node j, we have the time required for interprocessor communication c_{ij}, should i be assigned to the host and j to a satellite. The edges of the assignment graph can be doubly weighted with these times so that the SB weight of each path equals the time taken by the corresponding assignment (Bokhari 87).

It remains to apply the optimal SB path algorithm to this graph between nodes A and H to obtain the optimal SB path and hence the assignment that minimizes the larger of the load on the host and the worst load on any satellite.

The assignment graph for this case is a *multigraph* (i.e. more than one edge connects the same pair of nodes). A program tree with m nodes and f leaf nodes, yields an assignment graph with $f+1$ nodes and m edges. With the addition of dummy nodes and edges, this multigraph can be transformed into a conventional graph with no more than $2m$ nodes and m edges. The optimal SB path algorithm therefore takes $O(m^2 \log m)$ time to find the optimal path.

To account for limited memory on the identical satellites we can delete all assignment graph edges that separate subtrees with total memory requirements greater than the capacity of the satellites.

6.7. Summary

The SB path algorithm presented in this section is a generalization of the classical shortest path and bottleneck path algorithms. We have shown how this algorithm can be used to solve a variety of problems. The most important problem solved in this Chapter is that of finding the optimal global assignment in a single host-multiple satellite system. The solution to this problem combines the results of Chapters 3, 4 and 5. The SB path algorithm is a recent development and it is likely that it will find applications in many other problems.

CHAPTER 7
Mapping for Parallel Processing

The assignment problems discussed so far in this book have involved the placement of the modules of a serial or parallel program on the processors of a multiple computer system. The objective when making these assignments is to minimize some measure of resource usage. Most often the objective is to minimize the total run time of a program by minimizing the sum of execution and interprocessor communication times. The modules of the distributed program could be collections of procedures, possibly individual procedures, or could be data files.

In this chapter we will turn our attention to a specialized form of the assignment problem in which we are concerned exclusively with parallel programs. Each processor executes essentially the same program and the entity that is partitioned is the data on which the processing is to be done.

7.1. The Parallel Processing Environment

We will consider multicomputer systems made up of identical processors that are interconnected in some fashion. Each processor executes essentially the same program but on a different portion of the total set of data. The objective, of course, is to exploit parallelism to minimize the time required for the entire computation. The processors may be connected to each other according to a regular pattern, though this is not strictly necessary. What is important is the connectivity of the system, that is the structure of the graph that describes the processor-to-processor interconnections. Ideally we would like to have each processor connected to every other processor. In this case the graph of the n processor multicomputer would be *complete*: each processor would be connected to $n-1$ other processors. In such a system there would exist a direct communication link between every pair of processors.

In actual practice, such a completely connected multicomputer system is possible only for very small values of n. This is because such a rich interconnection structure requires each processor to have $n-1$ ports for an n processor system. The number of ports in a processor must increase linearly with the number of processors in the system. This is a very difficult requirement to satisfy. To appreciate this, consider the problem of completely connecting a 100 processor system. Each processor would need to be connected to 99 other processors and there would be a total of (100×99)/2=4950 cables in the system. For this reason, most large multicomputer systems are *incompletely connected*. In such systems, two processors that do not have a direct communication link between them must communicate by forwarding messages through intermediate processors. The communication overhead so incurred degrades the performance of the system.

The limitation on the number of ports per processor has led researchers to investigate numerous interconnection structures. The objective has been to design multiple computer systems in which the number of ports on each processor is either fixed at some constant value that is independent of the size of the system, or increases at a rate less than the number of processors (e.g. logarithmically).

One of the most famous examples of such structures is the Illiac-IV computer (Barnes et al. 68) that was installed at NASA Ames Research Center and which had essentially a 4 nearest-neighbor (4nn) connection as shown in Figure 7.1 This interconnection scheme is useful for

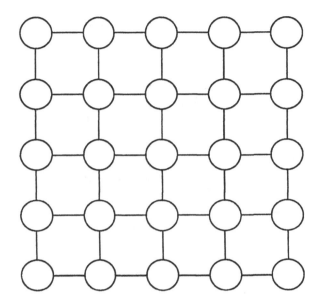

Figure 7.1 The 4 nearest-neighbor interconnection pattern.

computing many problems in physics and engineering. Notice that the number of ports per processor is fixed at 4, but the number of processors can be as large as desired. While the original Illiac-IV (which had 64 processors) has been dismantled, the 4nn interconnection structure lives on, most notably in the PAX series of machines at Tsukuba University (Hoshino et al. 83), (Hoshino 86).

Figure 7.2 shows an 8 nearest-neighbor (8nn) array, a real example of which is the Finite Element Machine (FEM) developed at NASA Langley Research Center (Jordan 78). This machine has been designed especially for structural analysis using the Finite Element method, for which the rich 8nn connection is useful.

Machines such as the Illiac-IV, PAX and FEM are called ''array processors'' because the individual machines may be imagined as being located at integer coordinates in two-dimensional space. Their interconnection structures are called ''nearest neighbor'' because each processor can be considered to be connected to its 4 or 8 ''nearest neighbors.''

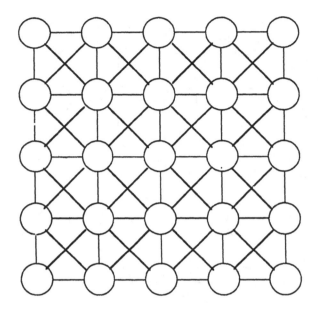

Figure 7.2 The 8 nearest-neighbor interconnection pattern.

The 4nn and 8nn arrays described above are inherently two-dimensional. A ring or chain of processors can be considered a one-dimensional array. Extensions to three or higher dimensions are obvious. A problem with such extensions is that their diameter (i.e. the maximum distance between any two processors) is proportional to $n^{1/d}$ where d is the dimension of the array and n the number of processors. The diameter determines the maximum time required to communicate between any two processors and is thus an important (though not the only) measure of a system's performance.

The *hypercube* interconnection structure has a better diameter of $O(logn)$ but at the cost of a logarithmically increasing number of ports. Figure 7.3 shows how successively larger hypercubes are constructed. A hypercube of dimension 1 is simply two processors connected by a single communication link. A hypercube of dimension 2 is obtained by taking two hypercubes of dimension 1 and connecting together pairs of corresponding processors. A hypercube of dimension d has exactly 2^d

processors with d ports each and has diameter d.

The field of interconnection networks is vast and well documented in the literature (Wu & Feng 84). We have mentioned only a few interconnection structures that are of relevance to the present chapter. Many other structures exist and new ones are continually being developed.

The first problem that we consider is that of assigning the nodes a given computation graph over the nodes of a given multicomputer system in order to minimize communication overhead. This *mapping problem* arises in many environments, for example when solving structural engineering problems. In Section 7.2 we will show that this is a very difficult problem for which no fully satisfactory solution is known at this time. We will describe a heuristic technique for its solution.

The second problem is that of partitioning an area on which computation is to be done (the *computational domain*) over the processors of a parallel system. If the domain is uniform (i.e. the amount of computation required per unit area is constant throughout) then this problem is straightforward. When non-uniform domains are involved, it is

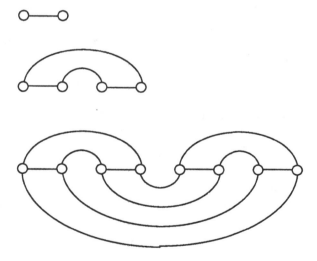

Figure 7.3 Hypercubes of dimension 1, 2 and 3.

important to ensure that each processor has, as far as possible, the same amount of load on it. In Section 7.3, we will describe a binary dissection strategy for this problem. We conclude this chapter by surveying some related research.

7.2. The Mapping Problem

7.2.1. Definitions

Suppose we wish to run a parallel computation on an array of processors. Our parallel computation is modeled by a problem graph G_p which describes the way in which various parts of the computation communicate with each other. The parallel processor or array is similarly modeled by a graph G_a which describes the interconnection structure of the processors. We assume that the number of nodes in the two graphs are equal and that exactly one problem node is to be placed on each processor node.

If the number of nodes in these two graphs is n each, there are $n!$ different ways of assigning the nodes of G_p on the nodes of G_a. We call each of these ways a *mapping* of G_p onto G_a. Some mappings are better than others. To appreciate this, consider the mapping in Figure 7.4 in which 6 out of the 11 edges of G_p fall on edges of G_a. In this case the two problem nodes (5 and 2) from G_p are mapped onto the processor nodes (B and F). B and F are not adjacent—there is no *direct* link between them. When 5 and 2 communicate with each other, the information must be forwarded through intermediate processors. This obviously takes more time than communication between problem nodes 1 and 5 which are mapped onto adjacent processors A and B.

A measure of the quality of a mapping is the number of edges of the problem graph G_p that are mapped onto edges of the array graph G_a. We call this number the *cardinality* of the mapping. The cardinality of the mapping shown in Figure 7.4 is 6. The cardinality of a mapping cannot, of course, exceed the number of edges in G_p. A mapping that achieves this maximum is called a *perfect mapping*. It must be borne in mind that a perfect mapping is not always possible. Figure 7.5 shows a better mapping of the same problem on the same processor array. This mapping has cardinality 8.

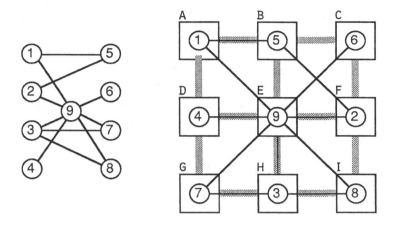

Figure 7.4 Mapping a problem graph G_p onto an array G_a.

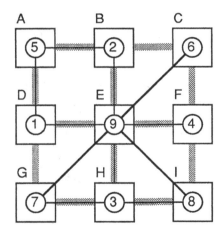

Figure 7.5 A better mapping of the problem graph shown in Figure 7.4.

7.2.2. Applications

The notion of mapping a problem graph onto an array graph finds applications in many different areas. An interesting application is from the area of structural analysis. When analyzing physical structures such as those that are used in buildings, aircraft or ships, structural elements are modeled by graph edges and the joints at which these edges meet are represented by nodes. Forces applied to one node are transmitted via edges to other nodes. Such problems can be solved on parallel arrays of processors by mapping the graph of the structure on the graph of the array. Since there is a need for transfer of information between problem nodes that are connected with edges, it is important that the mapping be such that as many edges as possible of the problem graph fall on edges of the array graph.

Figure 7.6 shows a typical structure and its problem graph. Figure 7.7 shows a mapping of the problem graph onto the 8nn FEM.

7.2.3. Relation to Graph Isomorphism

The mapping problem is closely related to the Graph Isomorphism problem. Two graphs G_1 and G_2 are *isomorphic* if they have the same number of nodes, the same number of edges, and if G_1 can be mapped onto G_2 such that every edge of G_1 falls on an edge of G_2 and every edge of G_2 has an edge from G_1 falling on it (Deo 74). The problem of establishing if two graphs are isomorphic is one of the classical

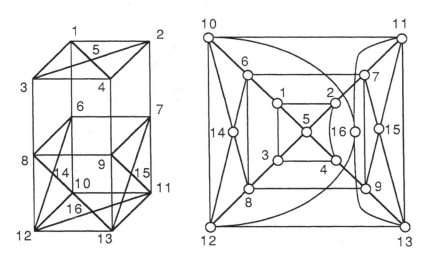

Figure 7.6 A typical structure and its problem graph.

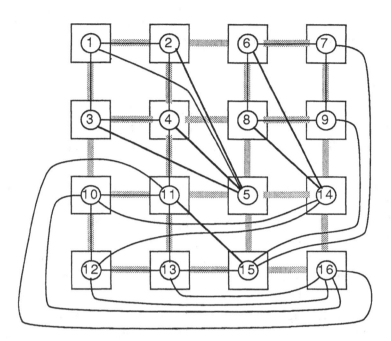

Figure 7.7 The structure of Figure 7.6 mapped onto a 16 node FEM.

unsolved problems from graph theory. Although it can be solved efficiently for certain restricted types of graphs (Leuker & Booth 79) a polynomial algorithm for arbitrary graphs is not known (Hoffman 82).

If we reflect on the similarity between the graph isomorphism and mapping problems, we soon realize that an efficient solution to the mapping problem implies an efficient solution to the isomorphism problem. This is because if two graphs are isomorphic they must have the same numbers of nodes and edges. Given an algorithm for solving the mapping problem, we can establish if two graphs (with equal numbers of nodes and edges) are isomorphic by attempting to map one onto the other. If the mapping obtained is perfect, that is its cardinality is equal to the number of edges, we can deduce that the two graphs are isomorphic.

Since no efficient algorithm for the isomorphism problem is known, although this problem has been studied intensively for many decades (Corneil & Read 77), we do not hold much hope for finding an efficient solution to the mapping problem. The mapping problem also has strong similarities with some other unsolved problems as discussed in (Bokhari 81a).

7.2.4. A Heuristic algorithm

Bokhari (81a) describes an algorithm that has given good results when used to map a number of structural problems on the Finite Element Machine. This is a *heuristic* algorithm in that it attempts to find a good solution rather than the exact solution.

The algorithm proceeds by attempting to improve a given mapping by applying a series of *pairwise interchanges*. If two nodes p_1 and p_2 from G_p are mapped onto a_1 and a_2 respectively from G_a, then a pairwise interchange constitutes moving p_1 to a_2 and p_2 to a_1. For each node in G_p the algorithm considers all possible interchanges and selects the one that leads to the largest improvement in cardinality. This process is repeated until no further increases in cardinality are possible.

Pairwise interchanges are not guaranteed to find the optimal mapping. By this we mean that it is possible to contrive mappings that do not have the maximum cardinality possible and from which the pairwise interchanges described above will not lead to improvement. When the algorithm reaches a stage from which no pairwise interchange leads to an improvement, a random perturbation is applied to the mapping. This is a random remapping of some nodes that is done without regard for increase or decrease in cardinality. In almost all cases, the cardinality decreases when such a disturbance is applied. However if pairwise interchanges are again attempted after this disturbance, an improvement in cardinality often takes place.

How good are the mappings obtained by this algorithm? This in itself is a difficult question to answer, since the only way to check is to enumerate all $n!$ mappings to find which one is the best. Certainly, mappings that are perfect or close to perfect can be considered satisfactory. Another way to check is to use the algorithm to attempt to map a random permutation of the processor array onto itself. This experiment can be repeated a number of times and the spread of values for the cardinality so obtained gives us a good idea of the performance of the algorithm on more general problems. Results of such experiments are given in the original paper by Bokhari.

7.3. Binary Dissections of Non-uniform domains

In the mapping problem described above, we were given a problem graph and were required to map it onto an array. Each node of the problem graph represented an atomic portion of the problem which we could subdivide no further. We only had the freedom to assign these nodes to processors so as to obtain good performance. Let us now study what happens when the problem is given to us as a large domain of discrete cartesian points and we have the freedom to put as many points as we like on the processors of our system. The objective here is to partition the domain so as to uniformly load the processors of the array.

As an example, consider weather calculations. The data in this case are the measured variables, such as temperature, pressure, wind velocity, etc. at various points over the area for which weather predictions are to be made. This area would ideally be the entire surface of the earth. The time required for the computation can be reduced by splitting the area over which the computation is to be performed into sub-areas and assigning each of these to a different processor. If the number of data points per unit area is uniform, the calculations being performed at each point are exactly the same, and the interconnection structure of the parallel processing system matches the communication structure of the problem, it is straightforward to assign sub-areas to processors.

In actual practice, however, the number of points per unit area may not be uniform because we may need higher resolution in some areas than in others. Similarly, different types of computations may be carried out in different areas. For example, in the case of the weather problem, we may choose to use different algorithms over land than over the sea. This introduces *variability* in our computational requirements. A uniform partition of the area is no longer adequate since it would cause some processors to be more heavily loaded than others.

7.3.1. The Binary Dissection Strategy

Figure 7.8 shows an example of the binary dissection strategy developed by Berger and Bokhari (85), (87). Each square in this diagram represents a computational point and the number inside each

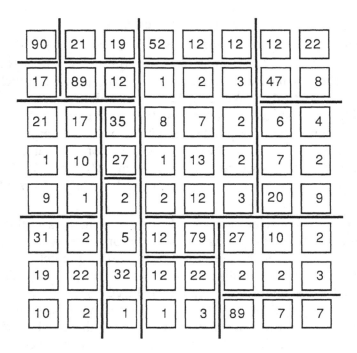

Figure 7.8 Binary dissection of a non-uniform domain.

circle represents the computational requirements of the corresponding point. Since our objective here is to describe the dissection method, we have chosen a small example in which each point has a different requirement. In actual fact there would be thousands or even millions of points and their computational requirements would be uniform over large sub-areas.

Binary dissection of the computational domain in Figure 7.8 proceeds as follows. We first draw a vertical line so that the difference between the sums of the weights on either side of this line is as small as possible. This is easily done by first summing up the weights on each column and then selecting a dividing point such that the sums of the column weights on either side of this point are as close to each other as possible. Having drawn this vertical line, we change our point of view by 90 degrees and subdivide the two halves of the region that were obtained in the previous step into quarters. This process is repeated as many times as required. In the figure we have repeated it four times to yield 2^4 subregions.

This process is called binary dissection because each subregion is divided into two at each step. We define the *depth* of a partitioning to be the number of times the dissection has been done. It should be clear that a partitioning of depth d yields 2^d subregions.

The partitioning of Figure 7.8 can be represented by the dual graph* of Figure 7.9. In this graph each node represents a subregion from Figure 7.8 and there is an edge between two nodes if and only if the corresponding subregions are adjacent. This graph is called the

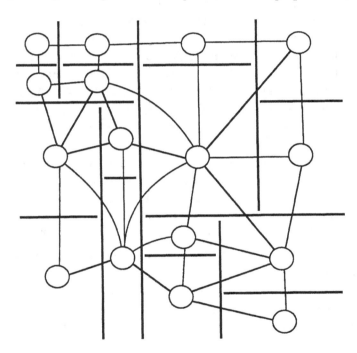

Figure 7.9 The graph of the partitioning of Figure 7.8.

*See section 6.6.1.

graph of the partitioning.

7.3.2. Natural mappings

Once the graph of the partitioning has been obtained, our problem reduces to the mapping problem of Section 7.2. Because the graph of the partitioning is obtained in a special way from the binary dissection of a computational domain, it has certain properties that make the problem of mapping much more tractable.

Since we follow a policy of assigning exactly one node of the problem graph to the array graph, and since the problem graph in this case always has 2^d nodes (for some integer depth d), it follows that we can work only with arrays of 2^d processors. We define a *natural mapping* of a binary dissected computational domain as follows. When partitioning the domain into two at the beginning of the dissection process, associate the left hand subdomain with the left half of the array and the right hand subdomain with the right half. At the next step associate corresponding quadrants of the domain with corresponding quadrants of the array, and so on. When the binary dissection process is finished each subdomain will have been associated with a processor. This is illustrated in Figure 7.10.

Berger and Bokhari (87) have analyzed properties of natural mappings and have obtained bounds on the cardinalities obtained when mapping onto 4 or 8 nearest neighbor arrays. These results show that for 4nn arrays the cardinality can never be less than 50% of the total number of edges. For 8nn arrays the corresponding figure is 79%.

The paper cited above also contains a detailed analysis of the actual time required to communicate when binary dissections are naturally mapped onto 4nn arrays and onto hypercubes. The analysis reveals that the advantage in using hypercubes is small unless there are very large imbalances in the computational requirements over the domain.

7.4. Related Research

7.4.1. Extensions of the Mapping Problem

We have defined the cardinality of the mapping as the number of edges of the problem graph that fall on edges of the array graph and have used this figure as a measure of the quality of a mapping. Other measures are possible. For example we may wish to minimize the sum

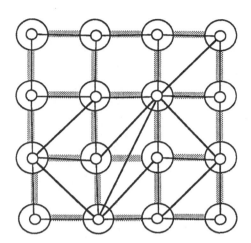

Figure 7.10 The natural mapping of the decomposition of Figures 7.8 and 7.9 onto a 16 processor 4nn array.

of path lengths between the nodes of G_a onto which adjacent nodes of G_p are mapped. By minimizing this measure we keep nodes that are adjacent in G_p as close as possible to each other when they are mapped onto G_a.

The discussion of Section 7.3.2. indicates that it is possible to find bounds on cardinality if the structure of the problem graph being mapped is well enough understood. Chughtai (85) addresses an extreme form of this problem. If we wish to map complete binary trees on 8nn arrays, under what conditions can we obtain perfect mappings? This question is of considerable importance because complete binary trees are the best networks for computing sums or extrema of data values stored one per processor. Thus, given an 8 nearest neighbor array which contains a complete binary tree as a subnetwork, we would use this sub-network whenever we needed to compute a sum. This is illustrated in Figure 7.11. Chughtai's work reveals that there is a limit to the size of an 8nn array that can contain complete binary trees. This is because a square 8nn array has diameter proportional to $\sqrt{N}$ while a complete binary tree has diameter proportional to $\log N$, where N is the number of processors. For large N the tree's diameter will always be less than the

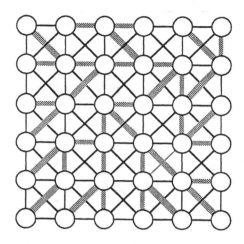

Figure 7.11 A complete binary tree that is perfectly mapped onto an 8nn array.

array's and it will therefore be impossible for the array to have the tree as a subgraph*. It is, however, possible to find perfect mappings of complete binary trees onto 8nn arrays for a finite range of values of N.

7.4.2. Other Interconnection Structures

The discussion in this Chapter has concentrated on multicomputer systems with "point-to-point" interconnections. By this we mean that if a communication link exists, it directly connects two processors with each other. In such systems, communications between pairs of processors that are not directly connected must be routed through intermediate processors that are required to forward messages as required. An alternative arrangement is to provide separate "switching" processors that take on the entire responsibility of routing messages. An example is the CHiP (Configurable Highly Parallel Processor) system developed by

---

*The subgraph S of a graph G that includes all the nodes of G cannot have diameter smaller than G itself.

Snyder and his co-workers (Snyder 82), (Hedlund-Snyder 82). Figure 7.12 shows one variant of the CHiP interconnection structure. The squares in this figure are processors and circles represent switches. Thick lines in this figure indicate communication paths that have been established by setting the switches.

The mapping problem for CHiP machines is more complicated than for point-to-point systems since an edge in the problem graph is mapped onto several edges of the array. Berman and her co-workers (Berman & Snyder 84) (Berman et al. 85) have studied this problem extensively and have developed techniques for finding good mappings. The problem of embedding trees in the CHiP has been studied by Bailey & Cuny (86).

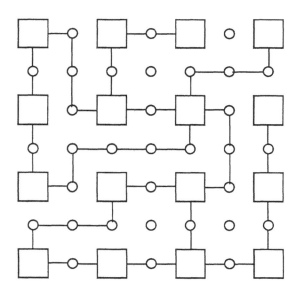

Figure 7.12 A 4×4 processor CHiP machine.

7.5. Summary

We have described the mapping problem and its variants and have discussed some approaches to their solution. The mapping problem is an important issue in parallel and distributed computing and is likely to remain an active area of research for some time. We have have discussed the close ties between this problem and the graph isomorphism problem. Recent theoretical developments in the field of Group theory (Luks 80) now permit us to test for isomorphism of graphs with bounded degree* in polynomial time. These developments have an important bearing on the search for an efficient solution to the mapping problem, at least for graphs of fixed degree.

---

*Graphs in which the degree of every vertex is less than some constant d.

CHAPTER 8
Conclusions

We begin this Chapter with a brief survey of alternative techniques for the solution of assignment problems. We then discuss the problems that remain open and the prospects for their solution. We conclude by describing the journals and conference proceedings in which the reader can find reports of recent research work on the assignment problem.

8.1. Alternative Approaches

Virginia Lo (84) has studied the problem of finding optimal cuts in assignment graphs for three or more processors. She has developed heuristics that find good solutions in most cases. She has also studied how the network flow approach can be extended to take concurrency into account to a limited extent.

Camille Price and Udo Pooch (82) discuss how search techniques can be applied to solve nonlinear assignment problems. Doty et al. (82) present a set of assignment problems and propose solution techniques based on dynamic programming.

Ashraf Iqbal (86) has developed an approximation technique for assigning modules to processors. This approach can be used to find solutions that are correct to any desired accuracy. Iqbal describes how his approach can be used to solve many of the problems described in Chapter 6 in time no worse than $O(mn\log(W_T/\varepsilon))$ where m and n are the numbers of modules and processors, W_T the cost of assigning all modules to one processor, and ε the desired accuracy. Iqbal et al. (86) describe the results of an experimental comparison of four algorithms for partitioning chains over chains: the algorithm of Section 6.3, a one-dimensional version of the Berger-Bokhari binary dissection approach described in Section 7.3, a greedy approximation algorithm from (Iqbal 86) and the predictive load balancing algorithm of Saltz (85).

8.2. Open Problems

We have seen how graph theoretic algorithms can be used to find efficient solutions to many assignment problems in parallel and distributed computing. There has been considerable research in this area over the last decade and many interesting results have been reported. Recent developments (the results of Towsley (86), for example) emphasize the fact that this is an active area of research and that we can expect to see more results in the near future.

The sum-bottleneck approach of Chapter 6 permits concurrency to be accounted for in certain types of assignment problems. It remains to be seen how this technique can be extended to more general problems. The analysis of Towsley's series-parallel algorithm under varying load conditions is another interesting area of research.

In summary, it is the author's opinion that the most fruitful directions for research in this area are those that emerge from a careful analysis of the structure of specific real-world problems. Realistic problems usually have many constraints on the structure of problem graphs and interconnection networks. These constraints often permit an efficient solution to be found for a problem that would be intractable in the general case.

8.3. Sources of Information

The major conferences that cover the topics addressed in this book are the following.

International Conference on Parallel Processing, held in the last week of August each year.

International Conference on Distributed Computing Systems, held every one or two years, usually in the summer.

International Symposium on Computer Architecture, held annually in the first week of June.

All three Conferences issue Proceedings which may be ordered from the IEEE Computer Society.

The academic journals that cover topics in parallel and distributed computing are as follows.

IEEE Transactions on Computers

IEEE Transactions on Software Engineering

Parallel Computing (North Holland)

Journal of Parallel and Distributed Computing (Academic Press)

In addition, the IEEE Computer Society magazines *Computer, Software* and *Micro* often contain articles of interest. The same is true of the *Communications* of the ACM.

The tutorials on *Distributed Control* by Larson et al. (82) and *Interconnection Networks* by Wu and Feng (84) contain reprints of numerous useful papers relevant to parallel and distributed computing, including many of those referred to in this book.

BIBLIOGRAPHY

Aho et al. 74   Alfred V. Aho, John E. Hopcroft, and Jeffery D. Ullman, *The Design and Analysis of Computer Algorithms,* Addison-Wesley, Reading, Massachusetts, 1974.

Bailey-Cuny 86   Duane A. Bailey and Janice E. Cuny, "An efficient embedding of large trees in processor grids," *Proceedings of 1986 International Conference on Parallel Processing,* pp. 819-822, August, 1986.

Barnes et al. 68   G. Barnes, R. Brown, M. Katz, D. Kuck, D. Slotnick, and R. Stoker, "The Illiac-IV computer," *IEEE Transactions on Computers,* vol. C-17, pp. 746-757, 1968.

Batcher 80   K. Batcher, "Design of a massively parallel processor," *IEEE Transactions on Computers,* vol. C-29, pp. 836-840, September 1980.

Berge 73   Claude Berge, *Graphs and Hypergraphs,* North-Holland, Amsterdam, 1973.

Berger-Bokhari 85   Marsha J. Berger and Shahid H. Bokhari,, "A partitioning strategy for PDEs across multiprocessors," *Proceedings of the 1985 International Conference on Parallel Processing,* pp. 166-170, August 1985.

Berger-Bokhari 87   Marsha J. Berger and Shahid H. Bokhari, "A partitioning Strategy for non-uniform problems across multiprocessors," *IEEE Transactions on*

Computers, vol. C-36, pp. 570-580, May 1987.

Berman et al. 85

Francine Berman, Michael Goodrich, Charles Koelbel, W. J. Robison III, and Karen Showell, "Prep-P: A mapping preprocessor for CHiP architectures," *Proceedings of the 1985 International Conference on Parallel Processing,* pp. 731-733, August 1985.

Berman-Snyder 84

Francine Berman and Lawrence Snyder, "On mapping parallel algorithms into parallel architectures," *Proceedings of the 1984 International Conference on Parallel Processing,* pp. 307-309, August 1984.

Bokhari 79

Shahid H. Bokhari, "Dual processor scheduling with dynamic reassignment," *IEEE Transactions on Software Engineering,* vol. SE-5, no. 5, pp. 341-349, July 1979.

Bokhari 81a

Shahid H. Bokhari, "On the mapping problem," *IEEE Transactions on Computers,* vol. C-30, pp. 207-214, March 1981.

Bokhari 81b

Shahid H. Bokhari, "A shortest tree algorithm for optimal assignments across space and time in a distributed processor system," *IEEE Transactions on Software Engineering,* vol. SE-7, no. 6, pp. 583-589, November 1981.

Bokhari 87

Shahid H. Bokhari, "Partitioning problems in parallel, pipelined and distributed computing," *IEEE Transactions on Computers,* to appear in 1987.

Bolch et al. 83

G. Bolch, F. Hofmann, B. Hoppe, H. J. Kolb, C. U. Linster, R. Polzer, W. Schussler, G.

Wackersreuther, and F. X. Wurm, "A multiprocessor system for simulating data transmission systems (MUPSI)," *Microprocessing and Microprogramming,* vol. 12, no. 5, pp. 267-277, December 1983.

Bollobas 79

Bela Bollobas, *Graph Theory: An Introductory Course,* Springer-Verlag, New York, 1979.

Burr 82

Stefan A. Burr (ed.), *The Mathematics of Networks,* American Mathematical Society-Proceedings of Symposia in Applied Mathematics, Providence, 1982.

Carstensen 83

Patricia J. Carstensen, *The Complexity of Some Problems in Parametric Linear and Combinatorial Programming,* Ph.D. Thesis, Department of Mathematics, University of Michigan, 1983.

Chughtai 85

M. Ashraf Chughtai, "Complete binary spanning trees of the eight nearest neighbor array," *IEEE Transactions on Computers,* vol. C-34, pp. 547-549, June 1985.

Coffman 76

Edward G. Coffman (ed.), *Computer and Job-Shop Scheduling Theory,* Wiley, New York, 1976.

Corneil-Read 77

D. Corneil and R. C. Read, "The graph isomorphism disease," *Journal of Graph Theory,* vol. 1, pp. 339-363, Winter, 1977.

Deo 74

Narsingh Deo, *Graph Theory with Applications to Engineering and Computer Science,* Prentice-Hall, Englewood Cliffs, New Jersey, 1974.

Dijkstra 59

Edsger W. Dijkstra, "A note on two problems in connexion with graphs," *Numerische Mathematik,*

142

vol. 1, pp. 269-271, 1959.

Dinic 70   E. A. Dinic, "Algorithm for the solution of a problem of maximum flow in a network with power estimation," *Soviet Mathematics: Doklady*, vol. 11, no. 5, pp. 1277-1280, 1970.

Doty et al. 82   K. W. Doty, P. L. McEntire, and J. G. O'Reilly, "Task allocation in a distributed computer system," *Proceedings of the IEEE Infocom 82*, pp. 33-38, 1982.

Edmonds-Karp 72   Jack Edmonds and Richard M. Karp, "Theoretical improvements in algorithmic efficiency for network flow algorithms," *Journal of the ACM*, vol. 19, no. 2, pp. 248-264, April 1972.

Eisner-Severance 76   Mark J. Eisner and Dennis G. Severance, "Mathematical techniques for efficient record segmentation in large databases," *Journal of the ACM*, vol. 23, no. 4, pp. 619-635, October 1976.

Even 73   Shimon Even, *Algorithmic Combinatorics*, Macmillan, New York, 1973.

Even 79   Shimon Even, *Graph Algorithms*, Computer Science Press, Potomac, Maryland, 1979.

Foley-van Dam 82   James D. Foley and Andries van Dam, *Fundamentals of Interactive Computer Graphics*, Addison-Wesley, Reading, Massachusetts, 1982.

Ford-Fulkerson 62   L. R. Ford and D. R. Fulkerson, *Flows in Networks*, Princeton University Press, Princeton, New Jersey, 1962.

Garey-Johnson 79   Michael R. Garey and David S. Johnson, *Comput-
                      ers and Intractability,* W. H. Freeman, New York,
                      1979.

Gursky 77   M. Gursky, Private Communication, 1977.

Gusfield 83   Dan Gusfield, "Parametric combinatorial comput-
                      ing and a problem of program module distribu-
                      tion," *Journal of the ACM,* vol. 30, no. 3, pp.
                      551-563, July 1983.

Harary 69   Frank Harary, *Graph Theory,* Addison-Wesley,
                      Reading, Massachusetts, 1969.

Hedlund-Snyder 82   Kye S. Hedlund and Lawrence Snyder, "Wafer
                      scale integration of configurable highly parallel
                      (CHiP) processors," *Proceedings of the 1982
                      International Conference on Parallel Processing,*
                      pp. 262-264, August 1982.

Hoffman 82   Christoph M. Hoffmann, in *Group-Theoretic
                      Algorithms and Graph Isomorphism,* Springer-
                      Verlag, Berlin, 1982.

Hoshino et al. 83   T. Hoshino, T. Shirakawa, T. Kamimura, T.
                      Kageyama, K. Takenouochi, H. Abe, S. Sekigu-
                      chi, Y. Oyanagi, and K. Toshio, "Highly parallel
                      processor array 'PAX' for wide scientific applica-
                      tions," *Proceedings of the 1983 International
                      Conference on Parallel Processing,* pp. 95-105,
                      August 1983.

Hoshino 86   Tsutomo Hoshino, "An invitation to the world of
                      PAX," *IEEE Computer,* vol. 19, pp. 68-79, May
                      1986.

Hu 82   Te Chiang Hu, in *Combinatorial Algorithms,* Addison-Wesley, Reading, MA, 1982.

Iqbal 86   M. Ashraf Iqbal, "Approximate algorithms for partitioning and assignment problems," ICASE Report 86-40 NASA Contractor Report 178130, June 1986.

Iqbal et al. 86   M. Ashraf Iqbal, Joel H. Saltz, and Shahid H. Bokhari, "A comparative analysis of static and dynamic load balancing strategies," *Proceedings of the 1986 International Conference on Parallel Processing,* pp. 1040-1047, August 1986.

Jordan 78   Harry F. Jordan, "A special purpose architecture for finite element analysis," *Proceedings of the 1978 International Conference on Parallel Processing,* pp. 263-266, August 1978.

Karzanov 74   A. V. Karzanov, "Determining the maximal flow in a network by the method of preflows," *Soviet Mathematics: Doklady,* vol. 15, no. 2, pp. 434-437, 1974.

Larson et al. 82   Robert E. Larson, Paul E. McIntyre, and John G. O'Reilly, *Tutorial: Distributed Control,* IEEE Computer Society Press, Silver Spring, MD, 1982.

Lawler 76   Eugene L. Lawler, *Combinatorial Optimization: Networks and Matroids,* Holt, Rinehart and Winston, New York, 1976.

Leuker-Booth 79   George S. Leuker and Kellogg S. Booth, "A linear time algorithm for deciding interval graph isomorphism," *Journal of the ACM,* vol. 26, pp. 183-195, 1979.

Lo 84   Virginia M. Lo, "Heuristic algorithms for task assignments in distributed systems," *Proceedings of the 4th International Conference on Distributed Processing Systems,* pp. 30-39, May 1984.

Luks 80   Eugene M. Luks, "Isomorphism of graphs of bounded valence can be tested in polynomial time," *Journal of Computers and System Sciences,* vol. 25, pp. 42-65, 1980.

Matelan 85   Nicolas Matelan, "The Flex/32 MultiComputer," *Proceedings of the 12th International Symposium on Computer Architecture,* pp. 209-213, June 1985.

Metcalfe-Boggs 76   Robert M. Metcalfe and David R. Boggs, "Ethernet: distributed packet switching for local computer networks," *Communications of the ACM,* vol. 19, pp. 395-404, July, 1976.

Michel-van Dam 76   Janet Michel and Andries van Dam, "Experience with distributed processing on a host/satellite system," *Computer Graphics (SIGGRAPH Newsletter), vol. 10, no. 2, 1976.*

Price-Pooch 82   Camille C. Price and Udo W. Pooch, "Search Techniques for a nonlinear multiprocessor scheduling problem," *Naval Research Logistics Quarterly,* vol. 29, no. 2, pp. 213-233, June 1982.

Rao et al. 79   Gururaj S. Rao, Harold S. Stone, and T. C. Hu, "Assignment of tasks in a distributed processor system with limited memory," *IEEE Transactions on Computers,* vol. C-28, no. 4, pp. 291-299, April 1979.

146

Roberts 78   Fred S. Roberts, *Graph Theory and its Applications to Problems of Society,* SIAM CBMS-NSF Regional Conference Series in Applied Mathematics, Philadelphia, 1978.

Saltz 85   Joel H. Saltz, *Parallel and Adaptive Algorithms for Problems in Scientific and Medical Computing,* Ph.D. Thesis, Dept. of Computer Science, Duke University, 1985.

Snyder 82   Lawrence Snyder, "Introduction to the Configurable Highly Parallel Computer," *IEEE Computer,* vol. 15, pp. 47-56, January 1982.

Sternberg 83   Stanley R. Sternberg, "Biomedical image processing," *IEEE Computer,* vol. 16, no. 1, pp. 22-34, January 1983.

Stone 77a   Harold S. Stone, "Multiprocessor scheduling with the aid of network flow algorithms," *IEEE Transactions on Software Engineering,* vol. SE-3, no. 1, pp. 85-93, January 1977.

Stone 77b   Harold S. Stone, "Program assignment in three-processor systems and tricutset partitioning of graphs," Tech. Report No. ECE-CS-77-7, Department of Electrical & Computer Engineering, University of Massachusetts, Amherst, 1977.

Stone 78   Harold S. Stone, "Critical load factors in two-processor distributed systems," *IEEE Transactions on Software Engineering,* vol. SE-4, no. 3, pp. 254-258, May 1978.

Sun 86   Sun Microsystems, *Sun System Overview,* Sun Microsystems, Part No. 800-1300-02, Mountain View, California, February 1986.

Tarjan 83   Robert E. Tarjan, *Data Structures and Network Algorithms,* SIAM CBMS-NSF Regional Conference Series in Applied Mathematics, Philadelphia, 1983.

Towsley 86   Donald F. Towsley, "Allocating programs containing branches and loops within a multiple processor system," *IEEE Transactions on Software Engineering,* vol. SE-12, pp. 1018-1024, October 1986.

Turner 80   Joshua Turner, "The structure of modular programs," *Communications of the ACM,* vol. 23, no. 5, pp. 272-277, May 1980.

van Dam et al. 74   Andries van Dam, George M. Stabler, and Richard J. Harrington, "Intelligent satellites for interactive graphics," *Proceedings of the IEEE,* vol. 62, no. 4, pp. 483-492, April 1974.

Wu-Feng 84   Chuan-lin Wu and Tse-yun Feng, in *Tutorial: Interconnection Networks for Parallel and Distributed Processing,* IEEE Computer Society Press, Silver Spring, MD, 1984.

Yao 82   Frances Yao, "Maximum flows in networks," in *The Mathematics of Networks,* ed. Stefan A. Burr, American Mathematical Society-Proceedings of Symposia in Applied Mathematics, Providence, 1982.

INDEX

ABOUT THE AUTHOR

Shahid H. Bokhari was born in Lahore, Pakistan in 1953. He received the B.Sc. degree in Electrical Engineering from the Pakistan University of Engineering & Technology, Lahore, in 1974, and the M.S. and Ph.D. degrees in Electrical & Computer Engineering from the University of Massachusetts, Amherst, in 1976 and 1978 respectively.

He was a Research Assistant at the Department of Electrical & Computer Engineering, University of Massachusetts, from 1975 to 1978. From 1978 to 1979 and again from 1984 to 1986, he was a scientist at the Institute for Computer Applications in Science & Engineering (ICASE) at NASA Langley Research Center. Since 1980 he has been on the faculty of the Department of Electrical Engineering, University of Engineering & Technology, Lahore, Pakistan, where he is currently Associate Professor. His research interests include performance evaluation, computer architecture, and parallel and distributed computing. He has published many research papers on these topics, mostly in the *IEEE Transactions on Computers* and the *IEEE Transactions on Software Engineering*.

Dr. Bokhari is a Member of the ACM and a Senior Member of the IEEE. He received the Best Presentation Award at the 1981 International Conference on Parallel Processing.